SECONDHAND
AND VINTAGE

BERLIN

Delia Dumitrescu

Many thanks to Berlin's secondhand
and vintage shop owners who shared
their stories and passions. These were
invaluable to me in compiling this book's
narrative. It has been a pleasure to
treasure hunt and portray such a vibrant
and original scene.

Published by Vivays Publishing Ltd

www.vivays-publishing.com

A catalogue record for this book is
available from the British Library

ISBN 978-1-908126-17-7

Publishing Director: Lee Ripley
Design: Draught Associates
Photographs: Delia Dumitrescu
and Andrei Mocanca
Map data: ©OpenStreetMap (and)
contributors, CC-BY-SA
Printed in China

BERLIN
CONTENTS

Introduction page 6

Chapter One: **Clothes and Accessories** page 14
Chapter Two: **Books, Music, Memorabilia** page 58
Chapter Three: **Home and Interiors** page 86
Chapter Four: **Only in Berlin** page 116

Maps
Kreuzberg - page 136
Friedrichshain - page 140
Prenzlauer Berg - page 144
Mitte - page 148
Schöneberg - page 152
Charlottenburg - page 154
Neukölln - page 156

Index of Shops page 158

BERLIN
HOW TO USE THIS BOOK

Each chapter in Secondhand and Vintage Berlin has a theme. The first three are categorised by goods – Clothes and Accessories; Books, Music and Memorabilia; and Home and Interiors. Chapter four, Only in Berlin, covers the flea markets and those places specialising in nostalgia related to the days of the GDR.

The entries within each chapter are arranged by neighbourhood. Each includes a description of the shop or market, alongside contact details, opening times and a guide to the relative price of the goods, set on a scale from € to €€€ (from bargain to investment).

A section of maps in the second half of the book shows you where to find the shops and markets, with each trader marked by a coloured diamond. The colour of the diamonds on the maps corresponds to the chapter colourings. These maps also provide a link to the internet that can be accessed through your smartphone.

INTRODUCTION

'There has never been a society so obsessed with its own immediate past.'

SIMON REYNOLDS, *RETROMANIA*

IF YOU WANT TO TRAVEL BACK IN TIME, BERLIN IS PROBABLY ONE OF THE BEST PLACES TO DO SO. I AM NOT TALKING HERE ABOUT THE AUTHENTIC TRANSYLVANIA KIND OF GOING BACK IN TIME, BUT ABOUT THE CHARISMA AND GLAMOUR OF THE URBAN PAST, THE INTERWAR LIFE AND HABITS. CATCHING THE VINTAGE FEELING IN BERLIN IS A CAKE WALK. I MEAN LITERALLY, YOU CAN WALK THROUGH THE CITY WITH SYSTEMATIC STOPS FOR A SLICE OF 'KUCHEN'. IMMERSING YOURSELF IN TIMES PAST COMES EASILY HERE AND YOU ARE SURROUNDED BY THEM. YOU WOULD PROBABLY WAKE UP IN THE MORNING AND DRINK YOUR TEA FROM A SECONDHAND CUP WITH A GOLD RIM BOUGHT LAST WEEKEND FROM A THRIFT STORE, OR TOAST YOUR BREAD IN A TOASTER THAT BELONGED TO YOUR GRANDMOTHER, PUT ON A DRESS FROM YOUR NEIGHBORHOOD'S FLEA MARKET, RIDE YOUR USED, SLIGHTLY RUSTY BIKE TO YOUR CREATIVE JOB AND END YOUR DAY BY DANCING THE CHARLESTON IN A BAR. BERLIN HAS PLENTY INHABITANTS WHO FIT THE ABOVE DESCRIPTION.

Why? The city itself makes them like this. And it's not only about living cheaply, but also about allowing stories from the past to sneak into our lives. I wonder what tales objects could tell us if they could speak?

There is something about other people's lives and other times' habits that fascinate us. Voyeurism has hit the mass market and social networks together with online self-publishing tools are a proof of that. What if secondhand and vintage is also a cultural manifestation of voyeurism? When we buy something that has already had a long life and belonged to several other people, do we want to experience a piece of those times and those people's lives? What were their lives like? What hobbies did they have and what was their social status? Do objects really wear an aura and keep their owner's energy?

According to Simon Reynolds in his book *Retromania*, '... it is not only about the obsession, but also about the access to the past that was made possible by recording mediums: records, photographs, TV in other words media and video. Now we are savoring the past because we can! The event is subject to endless repetition.'

Berlin is also a transitional city. People from many nations come to live here for awhile and then move on to their next stop, leaving lots of stuff behind. Only the stuff stays. Berlin is a city made out of stuff. No wonder some people started to make a business from it. Secondhand and vintage has also grown because it reflected Berlin's lifestyle and that naturally opened up a huge market.

The city has many styles. It can be Bohemian, yet still keeps something from the mysterious GDR era, there are the burlesque shows and the glamour of the 20s which are popular throughout Europe. The secondhand scene here strives to keep this feeling alive with its material but also with its cultural offerings: the shabby-chic look of bars, the swing music emanating from a café, jive dance courses, swapping parties (where you exchange the clothing you are wearing with somebody else's clothing from the party), the lavender bathroom soap that reminds one of grandmother's cure against moths, people's outfits on the street (if you're a bit tipsy you might be confused and think you went back in time) or even the new shops with retro designs and dandy wear (thedandyofthegrotesque.com). See what I mean?

The secondhand experience in Berlin is unique because of the coming together of two existing cultures: the East and the West. Yes, one can still feel it! Westerners (and not only) are keen on tasting Eastern life, at least by using their designs. Berlin is one of the few places where real history is strongly attached to the secondhand objects and this and not only this, makes everybody own at least one secondhand object, no matter whether it's furniture or a vinyl record, a dress, shoes or all of the above.

The clash between old and new has never been so powerful and the 'artsy' scene of Berlin makes secondhand culture thrive. It means getting the-one-and-only piece, the special (old) patterns, mixing decades, wearing mom's clothes, wearing a different style from all the others and bragging to one's friends about what one found. Therefore, secondhand means cool in today's society and in Berlin more than in any other city. Travelers from all over the world come to Berlin with the specific aim of buying secondhand. New Yorkers say Berlin is the new New York.

BEFORE WE SET OFF EXPLORING THE SECONDHAND AND VINTAGE STREET SCENE, WE HAVE TO CLARIFY SOME TERMS.

SECONDHAND no longer means cheap clothes for poor people, but cool pieces for unique people. Through secondhand we also understand recycled designs, restored and reinterpreted objects given new life and function. In terms of time span, secondhand has a short one (1-10 year old items).

VINTAGE is about objects of desire, old iconic pieces whether it is furniture or clothing. It has become easier to find vintage items as one no longer has to dig in order to find them, but the selection and differentiation between vintage and secondhand is often already made inside the stores.

RETRO should be understood more as referring to the look of an object as the term retro can be used in referring to a new bicycle's design or to an old car from the 60s or to an ad in a magazine. It just uses elements of the past, recycling and recombining them. Thus, retro has nothing to do with traditional.

So, yes there is something about Berlin and secondhand, vintage, retro, recycling or whatever you want to call this collective sharing and curatorship thing and in addition to the shop scene, it has heaps of manifestations. One of them is the Photoautomat. The exact translation of its label sounds like this: pictures for lovers, grandparents, sisters, night party souls, unemployed actors, day dreamers, moms, painters, melancholy souls, marine captains, star catchers and finders. These booths were restored in 2003 and spread around on the streets of Berlin. They still use the technique to create black and white photographs that actually inspired, amused and fascinated people since the 1960s. It has now become a cult object: 4 pictures for €2.

Another manifestation is the BücherboXX, a traveling yellow phone-booth library. While you can no longer make a telephone call, you are invited to take a book and leave one in exchange. Built-in exterior benches allow passers-by to stop for a quick read. You would have to Google its location as the BücherboXX is nomadic.

Similar but different is the Givebox, where secondhand items of any kind await to be traded with something else. This enables strangers to share with one another and what is in the box is constantly changing. You are even invited to learn how to build a Givebox for your own neighborhood.

THE RULES OF THE GAME

Prices are always in relation to the category line. If we are talking about a store that has clothes and it is expensive, the 'expensiveness' level is not as high as for an expensive furniture store.

Roughly this means:

€ = €1-50
€€ = €50-250
€€€ = €250 and up

This book has approximately 160 secondhand and vintage shops in Berlin that fit the following criteria:

– Both trashy and posh-chic: Somehow not the typical secondhand shop that everybody knows about

– Mash-ups between coffee places, candy stores and secondhand objects

– Surprising, funny, beautiful, different, friendly, cosy with good quality merchandise.

As the scene is so active, I am sure you will find some new ones until we get to publish the next edition of this book so just enjoy the quest!

SECONDHAND SURVIVOR'S DICTIONARY

The Kiez = when Berliners talk about their 'hood' they call it kiez and it comes from the Slavic tradition meaning a settlement from outside the castle walls.

Altbau = literally meaning old building, Altbau refers to high-ceilinged apartments built before 1949 that have big windows, a balcony, wooden floors and original art nouveau decoration.

Gründerzeit = literally translated as The Founder Epoch, before the stock market crashed in 1873, Gründerzeit times were glamorous. In terms of architecture this means richly decorated facades and 4-6 story buildings. Sadly, after the wars, many of the façade decorations were scraped away to be used as prime material for new building constructions.

Jugendstil = Art Nouveau

Hinterhof = backyard. Usually it is shortened with HH and inserted after the number of the street. The backyards can hide theatres, cinemas, galleries, museums, shops, cafes and most of the time good street art. So, stick your nose inside!

Wohnungsauflösung = Apartment clearance (remember, any of them might give you a washing machine, dishwasher or fridge)

Ankauf&Verkauf = Buying and selling, these terms always mean secondhand.

Trödel =Junk shop

Antiquariat = Antiques shop

THE NEIGHBORHOODS

When it comes to fizzy atmosphere, Berlin has it decentralized. Here you can't just say 'let's meet up in the center' because there is no such thing as THE center. Every neighborhood has its personal characteristics and its own hub and this makes Berlin a city of neighborhoods.

Kreuzberg

A very curious fact about Berlin is that it has a very strong history of migration so you can barely find a real Berliner still living in the city. The rate of population turnover is 20 years ...so much about settling down, right?

Kreuzberg is the multicultural part, where immigrants network. In the past it was highly political and populated with squatters, with a very strong subculture scene and alternative lifestyle: 'who's not rebellious, lives the wrong way'. Shades of those times can still be seen in the political posters inside bars in Kreuzberg. Even so, the neighborhood is soon to be completely gentrified - locals, Turkish, curious foreigners and actors live together and share the cafes around. Bergmannkiez is one of the areas that fit the description and it is charming. The 'petit bourgeoisie' (aka people working in administration offices) were living here in the early 90s, owning rich villas on the hill of Victoria Park, now a place of great Sunday barbecues.

Friedrichshain

Administratively, Friedrichshain is part of Friedrichshain-Kreuzberg neighborhood, but culturally it is never considered as being the same thing. This was one of the first cool neighborhoods for students to live because of low rents and the large number of bars and cafes. It was also the area where many squatters occupying houses were evicted with violence. But in the past 5 years it has become populated with middle class creative workers and is the home of media and entertainment office buildings. Simon-Dach-Straße and the nearby Boxhagener Platz are the most dynamic parts of the quarter. Samariterkiez is also one of the key areas in the neighborhood, where creativity and secondhand shops abound.

Prenzlauer Berg

The place for more bohemian youth, hosts the oldest buildings in town that were not damaged during wartimes. Many other beautiful buildings from the beginning of the 20th century were left intact.

Prenzlauer Berg used to be THE place to be in the 90s, but the young and crazy artists grew old, started having kids and transformed this area into 'Pregnancy Hill' - a sort of lovely place where you go to breed and eat good cake. It is now full of yoga studios, mother and child shops and school bookstores.

80% of the original inhabitants of this neighborhood in the 90s have left. The 'normal Westerners' and even some of the citizens of the East, never came back or didn't want to come to Berlin because it was 'construction grey'. 10 years later, the situation has turned 180°, Berlin has blossomed into an international location. The whole area was renovated and the new lofts became a big attraction for the rich and for the people who moved to Berlin from abroad.

Mitte

The desire of people wanting to live in the city rather than in the suburbs, boosted gentrification, raised rents and animated the city.

Mitte is the fashion district with a sprinkling of art galleries. Rents increase day after day so it is like a lottery game to see who can hang in there with these new conditions. The poor and the cool have now moved to Schöneberg-Potsdamer Straße, an area that used to be a place of child prostitution and drugs but is now an emerging venue for street art.

Populated by international jet setters and digital nomads (usually equipped with the latest Apple gadget), Mitte hosts some of the best secondhand and vintage shops. Alte and Neue Schönhauser Straße are busy shopping streets together with the area around Hackescher Markt.

Schöneberg

Schöneberg is known for Nepal, bio food, 40 to 60 year old inhabitants and has traditionally been a location for the gay and lesbian community. It covers some of the most special and charming nostalgia shops in Berlin. When you take a break from shopping, you can go to Tempelhofer Feld Park, where the old inner-city airport used to be and skate, bike, run or just walk on the landing strips.

Charlottenburg

Charlottenburg used to be the going out area in the times when Kurfüsterdamm was one of the most glamorous avenues, filled with theaters, cinemas and artistic venues. Now, it is the home of high fashion houses and luxury brands like Louis Vuitton, Tommy Hilfiger, Prada, Chanel. Still, even at its 125 year anniversary, something of its charm has been kept and walking down the street still gives the feeling of the wealthy world.

Neukölln

Neukölln has opened its doors to over a hundred galleries and art spaces and transformed from a 'problem' neighborhood into a 'scene' kiez. This former working class area has been adopted by creatives, especially in the Weserstraße neighborhood.

BERLIN, ESPECIALLY IN SUMMER, HAS AN AIR OF FREEDOM AND ABANDON. IT IS CALLED SUMMER SPONTANEITY AND IT COMES FROM THE FACT THAT REAL SUMMER DAYS ARE RARE IN BERLIN'S CLIMATE. BUT WHEN THEY COME, EVERYBODY SHUTS DOWN DAILY LIFE AND GOES OUT TO PARKS, TERRACE CAFES OR LAKES. SUN IS NOT TO BE WASTED HERE.

IN THE DIGITAL, MODERNIST ERA THAT WE LIVE IN, MIXING AND COMBINING IS WHAT CREATIVITY INVOLVES AND THAT'S EXACTLY WHAT VINTAGE BEHAVIOR IS ALL ABOUT.

CLOTHES & ACCESSORIES

*Men's, Women's, and
Children's Garments
Hats / Bags and Belts
Shoes / Jewellery / Watches
Eyeglasses*

BERLINERS HAVE THEIR OWN WAY OF PUTTING THEMSELVES TOGETHER. THE DIFFERENCE BETWEEN WHAT INHABITANTS OF OTHER CITIES MIGHT CONSIDER WEARABLE AND WHAT BERLINERS ACTUALLY WEAR AS AN EVERYDAY OUTFIT IS CONSIDERABLE. BERLINERS COMBINE EXTRAVAGANCE, DANDY-NESS, TRASHINESS, LACK OF AESTHETICS OR OVERWHELMING AESTHETICS. THAT'S WHAT MAKES THE VINTAGE AND SECONDHAND SCENE SO UNIQUE AND VIBRANT HERE. MOST OFTEN, THEIR OUTFITS ARE 100% PUT TOGETHER FROM FLEA MARKETS, THRIFT STORES AND VINTAGE BOUTIQUES.

In fashion and wearables in general, the love for retro started in the early sixties accompanied or pushed by the boom in antique collecting. Fashion designer Barbara Hulanicki, whose label was Biba, is the one who shifted the focus of fashion from looking forward to looking back. She declared: "I love old things. Modern things are so cold. I need things that have lived" (cited from *Retromania* by Simon Reynolds). She is the inventor of fashion retro, the cyclical recycling of styles.

Like retro, vintage is traced back to the sixties as well. When bohemians and hippies decided to wear secondhand and it was no longer labelled 'only for the poor', vintage was born. "The word itself comes from the wine trade where superiority is measured by how old the vintage is", says Reynolds in his book.

Today, vintage consumers are curators of their own lives. Clothing is not thrown away or destroyed; it lingers in the world

as a statement against fashion and current trendiness. But what do you do when vintage itself becomes a 'trendy' cultural movement? You go to Berlin and start riding the trend.

The approach to wearables depends on gender, purpose and personality. With this in mind, I will introduce the concept of beauty by impairment that came about from a talk that I had with Virgina Newton-Moss, a vintage devotee from Vancouver. The idea is that in the past, women were meant to attract the male by arousing his need for protection, looking helpless and vulnerable in their dresses and high heels. But the modern woman who chooses to wear vintage is strong, independent and has to cope with stony pavements in Berlin that are only made for flat shoes.

Most of the current mainstream wear is mass-produced and shipped in from the Far East so you see the same things everywhere. Beside the fact that excessive consumption is not good for the environment, vintage is original and exclusive, offers a high quality fabric, and lasts more than ten washes and one year in terms of style.

Let's see where we might find all these vintage and secondhand wearables in Berlin...

CHECKPOINT & CINEMA

Mehringdamm 41
030 612 011 45
www.checkpoint41@gmx.de
Mon-Wed 11:00-19:00;
Thu-Fri 11:00-20:00; Sat 11:00-19:00
U6 Mehringdamm

Checkpoint showcases a variety of selected clothing presided over by a man who simply loves old things. 50s dresses and girdles, 70s shirts, old collections of Desigual, Armani, Benetton, hippie pants and smoking jackets can all be found here. No wonder the items are sometimes sourced for film and theater props.

COLOURS

Bergmannstraße 102
030 694 334 8
www.kleidermarkt.de
Mon-Fri 11:00-19:00; Sat 12:00-19:00
U6 Mehringdamm

 The biggest and oldest vintage store (I could easily call it a warehouse) in Berlin, Colours lures clients with 30% off happy hours on Tuesdays between 11:00 and 15:00 and hard-to-find designer brands like Cynthia Vincent, Mike & Chris, and Recollection. I almost got lost in the carefully selected, beautiful everything: shoes, bow ties, crazy party dresses, wigs and feather scarves plus some more traditional corduroy suits and skirts. Colours is the place to grab an outfit before attending a thematic party or just when longing for clothes from the past.

JUMBO SECOND HAND

Wiener Straße 63
030 218 966 0
Mon-Sat 11:00-19:30
U1 Görlitzer Bahnhof

Biggest shoe assortment ever: high heels, flats, kitschy, elegant, purple, red, rainbow?! You find them all together with carefully selected clothes and matching accessories at the mesmerizing Jumbo shoe mecca. Opened by a Turkish family more than 10 years ago, Jumbo is the place for a perfect vintage shoe experience.

KINDERSACHEN AUS 2. HAND

Graefestraße 1
030 693 961 4
Mon-Fri 11:00-18:00
U8 Schönleinstraße

Kindersachen is like a playground. I could have easily spent my whole afternoon there, playing with the hundreds of games and toys that were lying around. Founded because of the owners' ecological concerns, the store claims that secondhand clothes are good for babies as the chemicals in the textiles have been washed out.

LINDT

Körtestraße 16
030 691 791 0
Mon-Fri 12:00-18:00; Sat freestyle
U7 Südstern

The name is the same as the brand of chocolate, but only the sweetness has been kept. What used to be a confiserie in the 50s has become a funky secondhand store. The owner's love for vintage clothes strikes you from the moment you step in as the items are so harmoniously arranged. The original dresses from the 60s are the icing on the cake. Lovely place with reasonable prices.

ROSENROT

Eisenbahnstraße 48
030 695 183 49
Mon-Fri 10:30-18:30; Sat 10:30-14:30
U1 Görlitzer Bahnhof

This six year-old store offers vintage clothes from the 70s and 80s for kids, at very cheap prices. Where do the textiles come from? They are brought in by the people who live in the neighbourhood. They pass by every day, exchanging something old for something used but different. This is where I heard for the first time about special eco wool for babies!

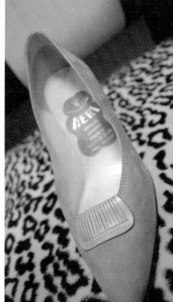

SECOND-HAND PARADISE

Adalbertstraße 17
Mon-Sat 12:00-20:00
U1+U8 Kottbusser Tor

Opened in 2005, this dusty store needs some attention. The owner loves cats so you will find her there every day accompanied by her four lazy felines. She provides 70s and 80s items, mainly shoes and bags, but also a large array of leather jackets. I'd say it is a place to check out, but be patient until you find your treasure.

ST STORE BERLIN

Karl-Kunger-Straße 54
030 53 21 23 05
www.schwarzetruhe.de
Tue-Fri 12:00-19:00; Sat 12:00-18:00
S Treptower Park

Even though this shop is slightly off the beaten path unless you live in the Treptow neighborhood, Schwarze Truhe is a strong presence on the vintage market scene. Paula started to collect vintage 10 years ago when it was less popular. Her closet couldn't hold any more clothes (typical!) and that's when she started selling on e-bay. The business worked so well that she had to open a store. She likes to be in contact with her customers: either older clients who want to rent 70s clothes for parties and carnivals or younger ones in search of real vintage to wear every day. Nostalgic grannies can dress their grandchildren in authentic 70s clothes, buy 70s curtains or Oktoberfest nuts can borrow a dirndl for the event. You won't find any jeans or t-shirts, but mainly cocktail dresses and special outfits with brocade or even wedding dresses! If you don't have time to pass by, no worries, they ship worldwide from their website.

STYLO

Hagelbergerstraße 52
030 604 011 78
funda@stylo-berlin.de/ www.stylo-berlin.de
Mon-Fri 11:00-18:00; Sat 12:00-16:00
U6 Mehringdamm

A generous store with clothes arranged by color and a nice smell – as opposed to the fusty odor in other similar shops. Bringing together both expensive and cheap items, the store sells Zara and Boss as well as no-name vintage, hip shoes, accessories and maternity wear. If you are tired after your long shopping tour, Stylo has a welcoming living-room-like entrance where you can sit and relax.

A&V MICHAELIS

Warschauer Straße 62
030 293 526 65
Mon-Fri 11:00-19:00; Sat 11:00-16:00
U1&S Warschauer Straße

Finally, a dedicated men's secondhand clothes shop! All sorts of brands like Carhartt, Diesel, Boss, Puma, Adidas, Pelle Pelle, Stüssy, Converse and many others, the shop carries suits, trousers, shoes, T-shirts and jackets. If something doesn't perfectly fit, they will adjust it for you.

BERLINER MODEINSTITUT

Samariterstraße 31
030 420 190 88
info@berliner-modeinstitut.de
www.berliner-modeinstitut.de
Mon-Sat 12:00-19:00
U5 Samariterstraße

Feminine, clean, colorful party dresses, casual clothing, handbags and shoes for which brand names are not a priority. You need to dress for a thematic party and don't know what decade to choose, where to get the clothes from and what items to look for? The Berliner Modeinstitut has various party outfits and especially 20s swing dresses. The shop owner and the historical fashion books lying on the coffee table will advise you on how to build an outstanding vintage outfit. If something doesn't fit correctly, she will tailor it for you.

GEILE JACKEN

Krossener Straße 24
030 782 784 7
geile-jacken@web.de
Tue-Fri 15:00-19:00; Sat 13:00-18:00
S&U1 Warschauer Straße

How should I put this? Tons of cool leather jackets in many styles. That's it!

HUMANA

Frankfurter Tor 3
030 422 201 8
info@humana-second-hand.de
www.humana-second-hand.de
Mon-Fri 10:00-20:00
U5 Frankfurter Tor

Humana is the biggest chain of charity secondhand shops in Germany and sells through 13 locations only in Berlin. I mentioned the biggest one in the description, but please check the website for the other shops that might be in your neighbourhood. Currently they mainly sell 80s wearables, classical suits, children's clothes and extra large sizes.

The association collects clothes from donations and this is the reason you will see huge yellow boxes placed on the streets in Berlin, Stuttgart, Hamburg and Köln. Humana also exports clothes to other countries, the supreme purpose being recycling: "We are committed to the redistribution: from rich to poor countries, of secondhand clothes".

JIBBOO

Bänschstraße 77
030 428 008 44
info@jibboo.de/ www.jibboo.de
Mon-Fri 10:00-18:00; Sat 10:00-16:00
U5 Samariterstraße

In addition to the extensive range of secondhand children's clothing, Jibboo rents items you need for a very short period for your fast-growing newborn, like baby backpacks or infant beds.

KLEIDER-MOTTE

Krossener Straße 29
030 203 180 90
Mon-Fri 11:00-19:00; Sat 12:00-16:00
U5 Samariterstraße

Freshly opened, the store offers first and secondhand clothing for children and women, complemented by jewelry, toys, books and carriages. All the items come from private houses in the neighborhood, on a commission basis.

OSCAR

Müggelstraße 11a
030 633 718 04
adirothkoegel@web.de
Mon-Thu 9:30-18:00; Fri 9:30-15:00
U5 Samariterstraße

A very tranquil and well-bred shop that sells clothes, newborn baby beds, books and toys, but only if they are made of wood. Everything is clean and in a perfect state no matter whether it is a brand or a no-name item. Loads of baby carriages were standing outside when I visited and I had a pleasant overall feeling about the place.

PARIS SECOND HAND

Samariterstraße 6
030 498 544 85
Mon-Fri 10:00-19:00; Sat 10:00-14:00
U5 Samariterstraße

Only one-of-a-kind French brands for kids. Chic fashion from Paris arrives in Berlin through this tiny and sweet shop. A stopover for German families from the entire country, this place is well known for unique designs and good quality textiles from France. Mais oui!

ROCKING CHAIR

Gabriel-Max-Straße 13
030 293 642 91
info@rockingchair-berlin.de
www.rockingchair-berlin.de
Mon-Fri 12:00-19:00; Sat 10:00-16:00
U1&S Warschauer Straße

Rocking Chair is like an escape into a world of comfort, warmth, creativity and inspiration. The owners are not only ideologically living the rockabilly life, but also visually and practically. They have surrounded themselves with things they love: vintage clothing, accessories from the 40s to the 70s and 20th century antiques. They specialise in vintage Hawaiian and bowling shirts, college jackets, Rockabilly, country style and 60s glamour. As far as I am concerned, the swimwear is one of the highlights not only because of its beauty, but also because it is hard to find in the stores in Berlin: high-waisted bathing trunks, bathing suits, bikinis, 50s beach dresses and 60s beach jackets. All items are hand picked mostly from the USA, but also from Germany, France and England.

SIR HENRI & MY FEET

Grünberger Straße 37&47
030 218 96 60
info@sir-henri.de/ www.sir-henry.de
Mon-Sat 10:00-20:00
U1&S Warschauer Straße

When you enter this shop you see so many Adidas and Puma cardigans that you might think you've ended up in an originals museum. Super cool old school! Remember the running shorts with a split on the side? Yep, lots of models are presented here along with motorcycle jackets, Levi's jeans and 20 year-old German army jackets.

Sir Henri has been attached to old things since he was a kid: "I enjoy old stuff in the same way as I like to listen to a good old song, and that's why I like to wear an old pair of jeans". This is the real vintage culture--a sporty shop with iconic fashions. The sister store, My Feet (at no. 47), caters to women and offers colourful dresses from the 60s and 70s, shoes, bags and hats.

TRASH-SCHICK

Wühlischstraße 31
030 200 535 26
www.trashschick.de
Mon-Sat 12:00-20:00
U1&S Warschauer Straße

For all you hipsters out there, this one is dedicated to you! Both for men and women, Trash-Schick offers very well preserved shoes, skirts and suits from the 60s. They change the collections regularly and adapt to what is trendy and fashionable. The most regular customers are English and Scandinavian, which may be because they are really about two years ahead of fashion, like the store itself.

ROCKING CHAIR

Ingo Zahn has a strong wish to differentiate secondhand from vintage, which I totally agree with. "Secondhand is worn and used stuff that you don't like anymore so you give them away to a shop in order to get rid of them. Vintage means collectible brands and items that you can't live without." I couldn't have said it better, though I believe one can still see the beauty in a secondhand item in which somebody else simply lost interest.

Ingo has been collecting bowling shirts since 1982 and used to bring home even the ones which didn't fit him. He just liked to have them because they were unique: "Vintage is a hobby and together with my wife I live my life revolving around old things: our furniture, our car, coffee machine and record player are all old. It is a way of life". Their whole lifestyle is about slowing down and going home for them is like entering the past. They create their whole environment in an old fashioned way.

Even the rocking chair as an item is connected to the grandparents, the name of the shop is inspired from *Rocking Chair on the Moon* by Bill Haley, rocking as in rockabilly and coziness. They have it all!

When they started their rockabilly life, it was new and underground but now it has became hip. It is a fashion scene and no longer a way of life. He clearly has it in his veins and his tattoos, haircut and glasses frame reflect this.

He is a profound lover of books on art, antiques and history and his favorite market is Rose Bowl in Los Angeles. He or his wife go there once a year because they can find the valuable, collectible items: "95% of the buyers today don't know what they're looking for but they start with dancing swing for example so they have a stronger wish to know more about the 20s and 30s and the whole culture and lifestyle revolving around that time. I support them in this."

The future is an everyday development. He lives with a constant challenge, that of making sure his customers find something new every week in his shop. His latest passions are work suits and swimwear.

He ends with a thought: "Old and new will come closer together because new cannot exist without the old. The proof is the special vintage edition of this year's Bread & Butter trade show where the new and the vintage are sold together."

'Old and new will come closer together because new cannot exist without the old.'

INGO ZAHN, ROCKING CHAIR

PRENZLAUER BERG

BLUE EYES

Eberswalder Straße 23
030 44 032 314
blue-eyes.berlin@freenet.de/
www.optiker-berlin.com
Mon-Fri 11:00-18:00; Sat 10:00-16:00
U2 Eberswalder Straße
or
Alt-Moabit 109
030 25 091 409
Mon-Fri 10:00-18:00; Sat 10:00-16:00
U9 Turmstraße

The styles of Audrey Hepburn, Buddy
Holly, Paul Panzer can be found at Blue
Eyes. An optician by training, Olivia, the
owner of the store now works with vintage
eyewear and sells frames from different
decades starting with 1920s. You have
a pair at home that is too rusty to wear?
"We recondition these little treasures and
transform them into real jewellery", says
Olivia. You want to add solar protection to
your glasses? It takes 20 minutes.

COU-COU

Winsstraße 31
0173 726 940 3
carmenbasiri@web.de
Tue-Sat 12:00-18:30
U2 Senefelderplatz

This place might fool you because you'd
never think it was a secondhand shop until
you read the labels. Maybe it's because
Carmen, the owner of Cou-Cou, worked in
cultural management. She stocks men's
clothes together with women's and kids'
clothing. You'll find more fashion items,
but no vintage, instead you get quality
materials and super beautiful outfits.

HILLY'S BERLIN

Kollwitzstraße 39
030 443 286 71
Mon-Sat starting at 11:00
U2 Eberswalder Straße

You're in a pony yard...traditional, country, crazy clothing and shoes for kids and women whether pregnant or not. There is glamour galore for the little ones: Petit, Palomino, Cosilana, but also basic underwear for newborns made of organic material. I'd say sweet and pretentious.

MEINS & DEINS THE REAL FLASHBACK

Danzigerstraße 38
0176 648 15965
www.meinsunddeins.com
Mon-Sat 11:00-20:00
U2 Eberswalder Straße

Cyclists and football fans, here is a store dedicated to you. You'll find original cycling t-shirts, Adidas football t-shirts from one to 40 years old. Apart from this, some motor jackets, jeans, pants and cardigans.

●●ⓔ
OPTIKING

Eberswalder Straße 34
030 473 724 88
info@optiking.de/ www.optiking.de
Mon-Sat 12:00-20:00
U2 Eberswalder Straße

Cat's eye, octagonal, Honni square, two-tones and other vintage eyewear shapes from the 50s-90s. The owner has been interested in eyewear since he was 15 and started to collect and later on to sell glasses at the beach or at flea markets. The business went so well that he opened an online store and then took over this nice space on Eberswalder Straße. 80% of the mint-condition frames come from Europe and you should definitely pay him a visit. You can still buy the glasses online and all the known brands are there, but in the store you might just discover a suitable no-name cool shape. Let's put it this way: it makes you want to wear glasses--even if you don't need them.

●●ⓔ
NYX

Zionskirchstraße 40
0177 9281005
angela.konz@arcor.de
Tue-Fri 13:00-20:00; Sat 12:00-17:00
U8 Rosenthaler Platz

If you know how, you can sew and modify the clothes you buy here. If not, Angela will do it for you or teach you how to do it yourself. Either way, you're not going to find vintage in this shop, but only 1-2 year old secondhand fashion, bags and shoes. Men can find a couple of dedicated shoe shelves with impressive models.

PAUL'S BOUTIQUE
BERLIN

Oderbergerstraße 45&47
030 440 337 37
info@ paulsboutiqueberlin.com
www.paulsboutiqueberlin.com
Mon-Sat 12:00-20:00
U2 Eberswalder Straße

It started because the owner always liked hunting for vintage clothing and sneakers. And because you didn´t need too much money to fill a store with it, he decided to open Paul's Boutique. It was named after the Beastie Boys album, reflecting its weird mix of samples and genres: "Strangely, only a few other people made this connection and instead everyone started to call me Paul! It´s a good name I have to say though, so I don't mind- they still call me Paul to this day!" says Paul.

For him, vintage is a collectible item that is out of production and he curates the items he sells by instinct and by following today's trends: "Everybody wants Acne jeans now for example. You look at the kids today and try to get it". And as young people love affordable fashion ...

Due to its popularity, Paul's grew from one space to three, each with its own focus. Oderbergerstraße hosts two shops. Goo sells used designer brands: Acne, A.P.C., Miu Miu, Dior, Chanel, Bernhard Willhelm, Marc Jacobs, McQueen, YSL, Y-3, Comme des Garçons. "The Mothership" as they call it because it was the first store, is packed with sneakers, t-shirts, jeans and streetwear: Levi's, M65 army jackets, chucks, desert boots...things that look better with age from the 70s and early 80s. The third shop on Torstraße 76 sells Cheap Monday's new collection plus vintage leather jackets, Doc Martens and shirts.

Paul is a collector himself as you will see - the walls and shelves are filled with toy robots, boom boxes and Star Wars collectibles. He did it, he made his passion his profession. Hats off!

SCHNEEWITTE

Hufelandstraße 12
030 467 947 79
www.schneewitte.de
Mon-Fri 11:00-18:30; Sat 11:00-14:00
M4 Hufelandstraße

Schneewitte is a super cute shop located on one of the busiest streets of Prenzlauer Berg - full of shops and nice cafes so I recommend a stop-over or a break from your walking tour here. You'll find extremely good prices for the curated fashion brands included in this shop: women's clothing, bags, accessories, shoes, all from the 80s until today.

SECONDHAND

Kastanienallee 6
030 443 084 45
Mon-Fri 11:00-20:00; Sat 11:00-16:00
U2 Eberswalder Straße

I know, not a very precise name but...It is full of leather jackets at a very cheap price so motorcycle lovers should know about this one. What else? Adidas originals, old school cardigans, shirts and shoes.

SENTIMENTAL JOURNEY

Husemannstraße 2
info@sentimentaljourney-berlin.de/ www.
sentimentaljourney-berlin.de
Mon-Sat 12:00-19:00
U2 Eberswalder Straße

This journey is a fountain of pure nostalgia. Clean and hole-free dresses, costumes, hats, shoes and men's wear from the 20s to the 80s. Travellers from all over the world step inside this store, maybe also because of the atmosphere the owner emanates. She says: "I want people to fall in love with a piece of clothing. Mass production no longer offers you the pleasure of longing for an item but here you do, you burn with the desire to own it".

SOEUR

Marienburger Straße 24
030 328 91 52 0
nina@soeur-berlin.de /www.soeur-berlin.de
Mon-Fri 11:00-19:00; Sat 11:00-18:00
U2 Senefelderplatz

Imagine a shop full of designer clothing for women made up of items bought but never worn. All those mistaken purchases go into Soeur. No vintage wear, just one of a kind designer secondhand from today's luxury labels such as APC, Isabel Marant, Margiela, Marni, Bally, Balenciaga, Valentino. The jeans come only from Acne and the shoe collection is amazingly generous. One of the most glamorous secondhand stores Berlin's scene has ever witnessed.

'I love secondhand clothing, I am crazy
in love with old stuff'

NINA, SOEUR

Soeur

"I love secondhand clothing, I am crazy in love with old stuff". That's how my talk with Nina started as I was sitting on a vintage heavy wood bench (also for sale) that looked like it came from a grandparent's backyard. The enthusiasm comes from the things she discovers every day, that good old element of surprise: "Every day feels like Christmas as little treasures appear in my store taking the shape of luxurious clothing items. You simply can't take your eyes off them", says Nina.

The owner of Soeur hails from the music management business where she worked for 15 years. After she had a baby, the secondhand adventure started. She was a flea market freak and owned a sweet secondhand store for children, but now she is exclusively into the luxury business.

She always liked taking a peek into people's wardrobes and she is now doing this professionally. Meaning? Meaning she has a few clients who actually let her explore their closets and pick whatever she likes to pass on to a new wearer.

She likes to offer late night shopping evenings in the store and is passionate about her work and the luxury brands she carries.

STIEFEL KOMBINAT

Eberswalder Straße 21&22
info@stiefelkombinat.de
www.stiefelkombinat.de
Mon-Sat 10:00-22:00
U2 Eberswalder Straße

Walking along the sidewalk you can't miss this store and you shouldn't. It is a secondhand landmark! In the front, piles of travel bags are piled to make up the coolest shop window ever. Inside both stores--there is one for men and one for women--you will be overwhelmed by the size and choice. It's filled with real vintage clothing, literally thousands of shoes, hats, bathing suits and towels. The highlight is the large collection of boots consisting of various models up until the 80s, repaired and renewed before being put up for sale.

THRIFT STORE

Kastanienallee 67
0170 448 667 7
myspace.com/thriftstoreberlin
Mon-Sat 13:00-19:00
U8 Rosenthaler Platz

Located on one of the most hip fashion areas of Berlin, Thrift Store can be the place where you, whether male or female, find the missing piece of your sporty outfit. Jeans and Adidas shoes rule the place.

ALEX VINTAGE STORE

Rosa-Luxemburg Straße 17
030 847 120 08
www.vintage-alex.de
Mon-Fri 12:00-20:00; Sat 12:00-20:00
U8 Alexanderplatz

Secondhand clothes, accessories and shoes from the 60s and 70s.

This store will bring you one step closer to vintage aesthetic mastery. Why? Because of the extensive selection of stunning vintage clothes. If you want the authentic look of the 60s and 70s this is where you will find everything you need. Displayed by color and country of origin (Denmark, Norway, Belgium, USA or England), the majority are everyday clothes with a sampling of eclectic sporty outfits from Adidas and Lacoste, a few party dresses and the occasional luxury brand name in amongst the unknown.

If you're recovering from the night before's crazy party, you can sit down, drink coffee, and let yourself travel back in time. If your purchase is over €30 you receive an accessory as a present. Thoughtful!

ANTIQUE VINTAGE JEWELLERY OLIVER RHEINFRANK

Linienstraße 44
030 206 891 55
or@antique-jewellery.de
www.antique-jewellery.de
Mon-Sat 11:00-19:00
U2 Rosa-Luxemburg-Platz

Take a jewellery person, madly in love with antiques, who has studied history of art and has a special affinity for gathering unique items, and you have this wonderful shop of antique jewellery. Besides exquisite taste, the owner has created an environment to bring these amazing jewels into the light. The shops is very light and bright, I had almost mistaken it for a new one.

The little treasures come from Europe's 1750-1950 and the highlights are the 19th century Victorian necklaces and a wide range of predominantly English pieces, using the latest industrial techniques of that time such as the cut steel earrings that shimmer like diamonds. Other innovative materials are jet (a coal like substance) or vulcanide (rubber from Malaysia). Extremely charming!

BLITZ BOUTIQUE BERLIN

Krausnickstraße 23
030 755 288 89
mail@blitz-boutique.com
www.blitz-boutique.com
Mon-Sat 12:00-20:00
U6 Oranienburger Tor

The Ramones, Cheap Trick, Die Toten Hosen (interesting for the German readers) and other classic bands' original t-shirts can be found here. The store was opened by a music journalist and is an extension of his love for music. If you weren't able to buy the t-shirt at a concert because it was sold out, you have a pretty good chance of finding it at Blitz--along with hundreds of other vintage concert shirts. The oldest one? A 1977 The Clash shirt.

CALYPSO

Rosenthalerstraße 23
calypso@calypsoshoes.com
www.calypsoshoes.com
Mon-Fri 12:00-20:00; Sat 12:00-18:00
U8 Weinmeisterstraße

A shoe paradise with a multitude of styles, colors, fabrics and seasons. You have every chance of finding that very special pair of shoes you've been searching for years - 70s cork shoes, 30s army boots. Mainly 30s to 80s.

CASH

Rosa-Luxemburg Straße 11
030 280 965 00
info@apartmentberlin.de
www.apartmentberlin.de
Mon-Fri 11:00-19:00; Sat 12:00-19:00
S+U Alexanderplatz

Secondhand and second season designer wear. If you're interested in Moschino Couture, Rick Owens, Comme des Garcons, Jil Sanders, then hit the road to Cash! The entrance is pretty obscure so you might miss it. Ring the bell and the door will open to a narrow hallway that makes everything look illegal. Apartment, the big brother store is luxurious and caters high-end wearables. You should see both.

DAS NEUE SCHWARZ

Mulackstraße 37
027 874 467
contact@ dasneueschwarz.de
www.dasneueschwarz.de
Mon-Sat 12:00-20:00

Tanya Bednar was inspired to open Das Neue Schwarz by her father who has an antiques store in Vienna. As fashion is her passion, she combined it with her talent for choosing secondhand items--inherited from her dad. Most of the wearables she sells look unworn and are exclusive brands from Brussels, London, Paris, and Vienna. There is also a good collection of men's clothing and she has an eye for good-looking shoes.

Tanya likes to dress different nationalities and especially Japanese who somehow manage to be more experimental and extravagant. Keep an eye out for her shop, it is in the backyard of the building.

GARMENTS

Linienstraße 204-205 & Stargarderstraße 12 A
030 747 799 19 or 030 284 777 81
mail@garments-vintage.de
www.garments-vintage.de
Mon-Sat 12:00-19:00
U2 Rosenthalerplatz

Garments was opened by ex-film costume designers so I need to say no more about the quality of the curatorship. It all started when the two owners had difficulties in buying secondhand because it was hard to find quality items, so they created a place of their own: a clean, stylish, new-looking store that is home to materials with special patterns, a big mix of decades and a few trashy only-if-it's-chic items. "I choose by feeling. It has to be something that looks cool, that is rare, something I haven't seen before", says one of the owners. Inside the shop you will find both men's and women's wear, sorted by colors and the style can vary from trashy 80s glam to punk or simply colorful.

GLANZSTÜCKE

Sophienstraße 7 – Hackesche Höfe
030 208 267 6
www.glanzstuecke-berlin.de
Mon-Sat 12:00-19:00
U8 Weinmeisterstraße

Costume jewellery was originally intended to be fashionable for a short period of time, an adornment for a specific outfit. So, no precious metals or gems here. Although it was not intended for collectors, times have proven the opposite as today Glanzstücke offers many of these 20th century body decorations. "Costume jewellery is about the appeal, charisma and magnetism of the design. It also reflects the zeitgeist of an époque in a very specific way...whether it is ludic, serious or experimental', says the owner.

It all actually began when she visited the Portobello Market in London and came back to Berlin with 70s necklaces that sold instantly at the flea market. She went back several times, her business grew and today she travels all the way to the US and France to bring back the beauties: Eisenberg brooches, Miriam Haskell necklaces, cufflinks and tie bars, earrings and rings. Attention girls, you are going to need a lot of time to admire these 20s, 30s and 50s embellishments.

LUNETTES BRILLENAGENTUR

Marienburger Straße 11
030 437 394 65
info@lunettes-brillenagentur.de
www.lunettes-brillenagentur.com
Mon-Fri 12:00-20:00; Sat 12:00-18:00
U2 Senefelderplatz
or
Torstraße 172
030 20 21 52 16
Mon-Fri 12:00-20:00; Sat 12:00-18:00
U8 Rosenthaler Platz

Lunettes has never-been-worn, original vintage glasses and sunglasses from the 20th century brought out by brands such as Dior, Jaguar, Saphira, Cazal, Ray-Ban or Robert La Roche. Unique models, high-quality no brand no logo eyewear has caught the attention of creatives, designers, actors, young and old looking for classic frames they have seen in the past. Currently most wanted is the 50s Panto shape and the one Harry Potter is wearing too.

At the Torstraße store, the 1952 customized furniture for glasses bought from an old optician in Babelsberg hides 56 drawers x 12 pairs of glasses in each. Lunettes also recently started to produce their own eyewear collection being very successful in Asia and throughout Europe.

MADE IN BERLIN

Friedrichstraße 114 A
030 240 489 00
www.kleidermarkt.de
Mon-Fri 10:00-19:00; Sat 12:00-20:00
U6 Oranienburger Tor
or
Neue Schönhauserstraße 19
030 212 306 01
www.kleidermarkt.de
Mon-Fri 12:00-20:00; Sat 12:00-20:00
U8 Weinmeisterstraße

A large selection of shoes arranged by colour tones with matching scarfs. You may have to empty your pocket a tad more, but only for really nice things: vintage clothing and brands, sportswear, shoes, accessories.

Made in Berlin is one of the top three places to shop for good secondhand in the city and it amazes the shopper with the variety and quantity of items carefully displayed. Offering selected trendy clothes, it feeds the hearts of fashion addicts. Imagine an H&M, just filled with secondhand. There you go, that's Made in Berlin. Happy hour on Wednesdays, 20% between 10:00 and 15:00!

O.F.T.

Chausseestraße 131B
030 605 060 52
ohnefragetoll@web.de/
www.ohnefragetoll.de
Mon-Fri 13:00-20:00; Sat 13:00-18:00
U6 Oranienburger Tor

The entrance is rough and precarious, the grey concrete gives the impression of a ramshackle building. But succumb to your curiosity and see the eccentric hand-picked items inside: clothes, bags, shoes, hats, accessories, or anything else than one can actually wear as well as some objects for interiors. Hidden in corners: 80s Escada and Dior. Yeah, cool without question (O.F.T.= ohne frage toll).

'Glasses are very intimate, personal'

UTA, LUNETTES

Lunettes

Uta studied history of art and film in Frankfurt and her story goes back to her university days. She was writing her final thesis and the large amount of time spent in the library strained her sight so she needed to start wearing glasses. As she was into vintage, she thought of buying a pair of cat's-eye Marilyn Monroe glasses but, surprisingly enough, there was no place to find frames like this.

So she thought why not? Glasses are a design and a fashion object too, so these vintage frames should exist somewhere on the market. That's the first time the idea of a vintage eyewear business came up. She soon found a cool glasses cabinet and shoved it into her parents' garage until she won financial support for her business plan. Smart girl! She moved to Berlin and started with a 17 sqm store that was her entire universe for two years until the PR efforts succeeded and the business took off.

"In my subconscious I felt the quality, design and craft of vintage glasses for the first time when a friend of mine showed me a pair of Dior glasses bought at a flea market in Tel Aviv", says Uta.

All the glasses at Lunettes are in mint condition and vintage designed, mostly from the 40s and 50s. I then wondered if the story of the past gets lost if the glasses didn't belong to anybody before... but she has a good point: "Glasses are very intimate, personal, almost like underwear because you wear them close to your skin so it is important to have them unworn."

Since 2010 she has also started producing her own collection that sells very well in the USA and Asia. A TV star from Korea wears one of Lunettes' frames from their new collection and this caused a real sales boost for them. What happened? This frame model was a perfect fit for Asian faces. "When you design glasses you must realize that Asian people have a different nose and you can't imagine how much impact this has on frames". Moreover, I find out that in Japan, eyewear is like a fetish. Women like men with beards and glasses and one of her frames won the prize and title for Eyewear of the Year in Japan.

It is clear that in order to buy, people need to hear good stories. So after the *Mad Men* series was broadcasted in Germany, people came in and asked for the *Mad Men* look eyewear. Other influential springs were Tom Ford's *A Single Man* and Andy Warhol's milky frames. Tom Zickler recently bought a few 50s and 60s style frames for his latest movie production.

RIANNA IN BERLIN

Große Hamburger Straße 25
030 864 509 18
info@riannainberlin.com
www.riannainberlin.com
Mon-Sat 12:00-19:00
U8 Weinmeisterstraße

There are some who say Berlin has no 'real' vintage. I would say this is not true and I would send them to Rianna in Berlin. No, she is not using her voice but her sorceress' flair in finding the best vintage Berlin has ever seen. She's been selecting items for 25 years and had a secondhand store in Athens called Berlin. She recently moved to Germany to open a shop that addresses the real-vintage aficionados who have a sense for aesthetics and its value (aka some dough). The criteria: colour, colour, colour as well as good quality and prints like the ones from Hermés or Emilio Pucci (her favourites). In addition, she sells vintage goblin bags and other handmade bag designs created by her with old textiles. She also covers pillows with vintage garments. All sorts of beautiful things seem to be gathered here!

SOMMERLADEN

Linienstraße 153
030 240 499 88
johanna@sommerladen.com
Mon-Fri 14:00-20:00; Sat 12:00-17:00
U6 Oranienburger Tor

For fashion enthusiasts looking for secondhand designer-label clothes and shoes. Carefully arranged according to Johanna Mattner's fine taste, the clothes are in perfect shape and very inviting. Doc Copenhagen, Miu Miu, Picar, Marc Jacobsen, COS and other brands lie on her shelves. Having worked in fashion as a wardrobe and props provider, you can be sure you'll find something new inside her store every day, labels that were not sold out and limited series end up here pretty fast. Most of the clothes come from private houses, and people who used to live in the neighborhood but have moved still send their clothes by post.

Don't miss Do You Read Me?!, an artful project space and store, just a few metres away on Auguststraße and take a coffee break at any of the corner cafes.

STERLING GOLD

Heckmann-Höfe, Oranienburger Straße 32
030 280 965 00
info@ www.sterlinggold.de
www.sterlinggold.de
Mon-Fri 12:00-20:00; Sat 12:00-18:00
S Oranienburger Straße

Close your eyes and imagine you are
in the middle of a ballroom. Colourful,
princess dresses with lace and tulle float
around you. You're not dreaming, you're
at Sterling Gold. This dress shop opened
more than 12 years ago and offers a vast
collection of American 30s-50s formal
dresses. And when I say vast I mean any
color, for any age from young children
to 80 year-old ladies, cool and crazy or
baroque and traditional, opera costumes
or ballgowns and unique wedding outfits.

XVII OR DIX-SEPT

Steinstraße 17
030 544 828 82
c@xvii-store.com/ www.xvii-store.com
Mon-Fri 11:00-19:00; Sat 11:00-17:00
U2 Rosenthaler Platz

This store is a newcomer and it surely
brings refreshing and exquisite taste to
the vintage market. The women who own
the store are passionate about vintage
and pick the outfits according to their
gut sense, traveling to flea markets in
Italy and San Francisco, bringing mostly
80s styles. They want to change the
perception of vintage being only old-
fashioned clothes and show its cool side
by suggesting outfit combinations on
their Tumblr page. Spotted style at the
time: vintage oriental waistcoats. You'll
find a very different and special style here
compared with other stores. It's in the
top 5!

AUNES

Kolonnenstraße 3
0162 890 208 8
Tue-Sat 14:00-18:00
U7 Kleistpark

Aunes is originally from Denmark where she studied industrial design. Now she owns a shop that bears her name and sells clothing items and objects from 1900 to today. Belle Époque clothing, Art Nouveau jewellery and brooches, toys, porcelain and matchboxes make up a wonderful treasure trove to explore. The selection criteria: it should be fun and good looking. Inexpensive and organised by someone with taste.

FIRLEFANZ

Eisenacher Straße 75
030 781 747 5
www.firlefanz-berlin.de
Mon-Fri 14:30-18:30; Sat 11:00-15:00
U7 Eisenacher Straße

A lovely shop with 40s-60s wearables including beautiful American fashion accessories and interior decorations, small furniture items like chairs or kidney-shaped lamp tables. Hat and lace glove lovers, this is a store you shouldn't miss!

LUMPEN PRINZESSIN

Kyffhäuserstraße 19
030 806 143 68
info@lumpenprinzessin.de
www.lumpenprinzessin.de
Mon-Fri 10:30-18:30; Sat 11:00-15:00
U7 Eisenacher Straße

Very well stocked with clothing for mothers and soon-to-be mothers clothing, baby and young kids' wearables, books, tricycles, wagons, Bobby-Cars, cartoon DVDs and videos. They also have several locations so check the web to find your nearest one.

MIMI

Goltzstraße 5
030 23 63 8438
mimi@mimi-berlin.de/ www.mimi-berlin.de
Mon-Fri 12:00-19:00; Sat 11:00-16:00
U7 Eisenacher Straße

Mimi is Mirjam Grese, the owner, and her story starts with collecting hats. At a certain point, she ran out of space to store them and had to start sharing them with the outside world. When she started selling them at flea markets, a costume designer told her it was a pity to sell these rare hats and that she should rent them instead. That's exactly what she did. It was so fun and successful, that she opened a shop that over the past ten years has grown in size and range of stock. Even though the entrance and window look romantic and feminine, Mimi specialises in men's tailoring so don't be fooled, go all the way to the back to find bow ties, hats, braces, cufflinks, suits and tailcoats. Women are also spoiled with vintage items from 1880 to 1950: dresses, goblin handbags, cigarette holders, nightgowns and linen with clothes for children too. If this is not enough, ask for the 'fundus', that's where she keeps special items. Mimi rents outfits to vintage party aficionados as well. You're one of them? Google Boheme Sauvage Berlin!

SILHOUETTE IM FARBENREIGEN

Belziger Straße 19
030 787 120 38
Mon 14:00-19:00; Tue-Fri 12:00-19:00;
Sat 11:00-16:00
U7 Eisenacher Straße

Selling only secondhand clothing, Silhouette im Farbenreigen focuses on fashion and new styles, mass-market brands that are never older than 3-4 years. All clothes come from people living in the area around the store.

TROLLBY

Eisenacher Straße 78
030 375 874 45
info@trollby.com / www.trollby.com
Mon-Fri 10:00-18:00; Sat 10:00-16:00
U7 Eisenacher Straße

Trollby, come by to see the trolls'
backyard! This store has the most
creative interior design of all children's
secondhand stores in Berlin. As soon as
you step inside, you enter a fairytale land
where you are welcomed by a wooden
troll house, a reading corner and a playing
area. All this and very good prices for a
cool and wide range of items for
your children.

GARAGE

Ahornstraße 2
030 211 276 0
www.kleidermarkt.de
Mon-Fri 10:00-19:00; Sat 11:00-18:00
U1U2U3U4 Nollendorfplatz

A spacious basement with men's and
women's secondhand wearables. Being
the sister of Made in Berlin and raised in
the same style, Garage offers 30% off on
Wednesdays between 11:00 and 13:00 -
this means the price per kilogram goes
from €14 down to €10. Enjoy!

MACZY'Z

Mommsenstraße 2
030 881 136 3
theresiawirtz@macyz.de/ facebook.com
macyz.de
Mon-Fri 12-19; Sat 12:00 -16 :00
S Savignyplatz

Imagine two models opening up a
designers secondhand store! This quality
collection has been gathered by experts
who have been doing this for the past
25 years. Nothing more than 2 years old,
Balenciaga, Celine, Dior, Chloe enchant
the many tourists coming into her store.
Harmoniously disposed trendy and
beautiful luxury clothing, shoes (they all
look unworn!) and sunglasses.

MADONNA

Mommsenstraße 57
030 324 763 2
Mon-Fri 12:00-19:00; Sat 11:00-17:00
S Savignyplatz

The arrangement might not suggest it, but this place offers past collections of luxury brands. It is more about digging than browsing, but you'll find it rewarding. The collection of shoes is very complete: Manolos and Choos, check! More of a traditional and classical style for women.

SECONDO

Mommsenstraße 61
030 881 22 91
www.secondoberlin.de
Mon-Fri 11:00-18:30; Sat 11:00-15:30
S Savignyplatz

Here you'll find Versaces, Gaultiers, Chanels, Gabbanas and so on. If you happen to have too many designer items yourself, you can bring them here to sell on commission. This way your lonely luxurious piece of clothing will soon find a new owner.

Men are not left out and are offered suits, shirts and shoes. The collection is never older than 2 or 3 years and the style ranges from hippie to conservative. Opened 25 years ago, the place is almost a cult store, very well known by theaters and film producers.

TONY DURANTE

Suarezstraße 62
030 318 034 18
durantetony@hotmail.com
Mon-Fri 12:00-18:30; Sat 11:30-16:00
U2 Sophie-Charlotte-Platz

You're about to get married and want to do it in a vintage style? Then go to Tony Durante, he'll dress you in a beautiful 40s style wedding dress with a matching cape, offer a nightgown or lingerie from the same period, dress your bridesmaids in 20s, 60s or 70s cocktail dresses and adorn them with art deco jewelry. Men get special cufflinks models from the 50s and earlier. For the pool party, there are one-piece swimsuits and bathing caps available.

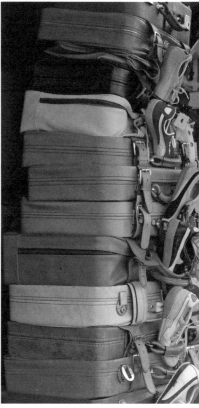

KLEINES GLÜCK

Weichselstraße 38
030 922 508 33
kleines.glueck@gmx.net
Tue-Sat 11:00-17:00
U7 Rathaus Neukölln

A mix between beautiful and almost unworn baby clothes and new hand- made items that can be given as gifts. Kleines Glück offers unique items. If the owner receives a simple t-shirt she wouldn't place it on the shelves before customizing it and applying something chic to it. The H&M and Zara baby lines are in very good condition and sold at a price agreed with the 'giver'. Sometimes evenings are filled with children's book readings or tips & tricks sessions for parents on how to choose carriages, etc. An absolutely lovely place, comfy and making any non-parents want to become one. Beware!

Kleines Glück

'children grow so fast that they don't even wear out an item of clothing. It is a pity to throw them away and buy something new.'

DANI, KLEINES GLÜCK

A very friendly and helpful soul, Dani Eigenwillig, worked as a journalist and always dreamed of having a gallery café or something similar that would create a comfortable feeling. After she became a mother, she realized that she didn't want to go back to being a journalist and worked for six months to develop the concept of a secondhand store for children. She found this lovely place in Kreuzkölln and with the help of her friends and husband, she bought the furniture, renovated the place and opened Kleines Glück.

The store and its character grew together with her daughter, who is 3 years old now. Dani's been in the neighborhood for about two years and practically knows the kids by name. She noticed that some materials tend break easily, but what she puts in her store are quality materials that will last for years: "Anyway, children grow so fast that they don't even wear out an item of clothing. It is a pity to throw them away and buy something new...we don't need so many new things", says Dani.

As you probably already know, Berlin is very neighbourhood focused and people rarely leave their locale just to buy something. Therefore, secondhand shops become locally popular. That's why Dani wanted to open the store very close to where she lives. In conclusion, "people who have a child for the first time buy too many things at the beginning and they soon realize that they don't need it all. Secondhand stores are a way to get rid of these items and replace them with something else".

BOOKS, MUSIC & MEMORABILIA

Bicycles / Vinyl / Art
Books / Cameras
Musical Instruments

ART, MUSIC, BOOKS AND BICYCLES ARE AN ODD COMBINATION BUT IF YOU COME TO THINK ABOUT IT, THEY ARE ALL ABOUT WELLBEING FOR BOTH YOUR BODY AND SOUL.

Art in Berlin covers a wide spectrum of interpretation and this may be one of the reasons why you can find it almost everywhere, especially at flea markets (see Only in Berlin chapter), piled up along with other objects rather than in a separate setting of its own.

Vinyl shops are easy to find and a wealth of good records can be found in almost every shop so nobody feels disadvantaged. Although Berlin's music venues are renowned for minimal, techno and house, its music shops seem to prefer mellow tones: jazz, blues, soul and funky electro.

For the book lovers, there are a myriad of antiquarian and secondhand bookshops that sell both oldies and goldies plus recent publications that have a flaw or were publishers' left over stock. Strolling the streets will make you wonder whether Berlin is actually in Germany or is just a meeting place for people from all over the world--with many English-language speakers. For them, as for us, there are always at least a few shelves with English, Spanish, French editions or even dedicated bookstores.

Bikes are must-have accessories in Berlin. Well, if you wish for the bohemian life you need to do it the right way. Owning a car here will only get you a weird look and there is nothing nicer and more eco-friendly than moving from A to B on a bike with the breeze blowing through your hair. Moreover, there are so many picturesque bike routes one can take that it would be a pity to miss them. If you live the secondhand and vintage lifestyle, then Berlin is the place and you will have your choice of plenty of old, rusty and retro bikes.

KREUZBERG

ANTIQUARIAT KALLIGRAMM

Oranienstraße 28
030-614 44 25
kontakt@kalligramm.de / kalligramm.de
Mon-Fri 12:00-18:00; Sat 12:00-16:00
U1+U8 Kottbusser Tor

Located on the liveliest street of
Kreuzberg, Antiquariat Kalligram offers
books from the 80s and 90s in a fresh
environment. The shelves have space
to breathe and the titles primarily focus
on theory and philosophy with a leftist
political slant.

BIKE:CO:HOLICS

Gneisenaustraße 67
0157 729 592 51
info@bikecoholics.de
www.bikecoholics.de
Mon-Fri 11:00-19:00
U7 Gneisenaustraße / Iwo Lowag

The enthusiast cyclists at Bike:co:holics
will undoubtedly hook you up with a cool
bike. The new ones hang on the walls
inside and the secondhand ones are
displayed outside. Lots of models
to choose from.

ART ET ANTIQUITIES

Zossener Straße 48
030 616 752 59
gbenker@t-online.de
Mon-Fri 16:00-19:00
U7 Gneisenaustraße

Owned by Guido Benker, a painter
himself, this little studio sells ethnic
and contemporary art, some pieces of
furniture and antique lamps every now
and then – depending on what Guido finds
at the nearby Markthalle flea market on
weekends.

EXTRA-BUCH: MODERNES ANTIQUARIAT

Mehringdamm 66
030 789 517 97
extrabuch@t-online.de/ www.extra-buch.de
Mon-Fri 10:00-20:00; Sat 10:00-18:00
U6/U7 Mehringdamm

The beautiful books you've always wanted, but with a modest flaw: teNeues, Daab, Taschen, and other interior design, manga, myth or medical books. While the books are not older than a year, they are books that have been returned to the publisher's warehouse, so they all look a bit 'tired' but the 50% off, especially for the art books, is irresistible.

HAMMETT

Friesenstraße 27
030 691 58 34
hamett@hammett-krimis.de
www.hammett-krimis.de
Mon-Fri 10:00-20:00; Sat 9:00-18:00
U7 Gneisenaustraße

Do you like being thrilled? Then Hammett is the place for you. Crime book lovers, this is your place! Hammett offers a large selection of books and does free readings from time to time.

FAIR EXCHANGE

Dieffenbachstraße 58
030 694 467 5
info@fairexchange.de
www.fair-exchange.de
Mon-Fri 11:00-19:00; Sat 10:00-18:00
U8 Schönleinstraße

Two English teachers, Paula from New York and Susan from Boston opened the Fair Exchange bookstore in 1984. Inside the cosy shop stocked with used English language books, you can find literature arranged in alphabetical order covering the classics to contemporary fiction as well as psychology, history, science, art, philosophy, biographies and film. Berlin is fond of its English-speaking inhabitants. And there are many!

KUBI'S BIKE SHOP

Falckensteinstraße 35
030 805 745 35
mail@kubisbikeshop.com
www.kubisbikeshop.com
Mon-Fri 10:00-19:00, Sat 10:00-16:00
U1 Schlesisches Tor

At Kubi's you can find really good bikes, carefully repaired and polished before being offered for insanely honest prices. Try to go there on Monday mornings, that's when they line up the best bikes of the week. In the high season the good models sell out very fast.

LONG PLAYER-VINYL LIVING ROOM

Graefestraße 80
030 34 74 83 30
contact@long-player.de
www.long-player.de
Tue, Thu-Sat 12:00-20:00;
Wed 12:00-24:00
U8 Schönleinstraße

This record store has one of the best rap collections together with soul and funk beats. The place is cosy and welcoming as if it were the owner's living room. He likes to sit amongst his records most days: This explains the extended opening times.

KULTGUT

Wrangelstraße 45
030 612 42 06
kultgut@googlemail.com
www.abebooks.de
Mon-Fri 13:00-19:00; Sat 11:00-16:00
U1 Schlesisches Tor

This place is challenging and cheap! Kultgut is a small shop that sells secondhand books on esoteric subjects, science fiction and film. It is worth a visit for the 1€ flat fee and...well...to see the owner's outfit.

MODERN GRAPHICS

Oranienstraße 22
030 615 8810
kontakt@modern-graphics.de
www.modern-graphics.de
Mon-Fri 11:00-20:00; Sat 10:00-19:30
U8 U1 Kottbusser Tor

Lots of *Marvel* comics issues and just a few independent comics. The issues come from private collections so you never know what you're going to find in the boxes. If you're looking for a 20 year old *X-Men* that hasn't been reprinted in paperback like the others, you can try your luck at Modern Graphics. Recommended for comics nostalgics!

MÜßIGGANG

Oranienstraße 14a
030 629 012 78
buchladen@muessiggang.net
www.muessiggang.net
Tue-Sat 14:00-19:00 U8
U1 Kottbusser Tor

I fell in love with Müßiggang because of its laid back spirit. Still keeping the old sign - Möbel Klitzke - the bookstore is watched over by a Space Invader mosaic installed outside on the left wall by the notorious French urban artist, Invader. Besides being a secondhand bookstore, the space also shelters a free radio station, a law office and a feminist association. Situated in the SO36 Kreuzberg punk district frequented by Iggy Pop in the 70s, the area is now a bit quieter but still has an edgy quality like the bookstore itself. The shop invites you to browse through books on politics, history, theater and crime. The owner can tell you many things about the history of the area, so don't be too shy to ask.

OTHER LAND

Bergmannstraße 25
030 695 051 17
service@otherland-berlin.de
www.otherland-berlin.de
Mon-Fri 11:00-19:00; Sat 11:00-17:00
U7 Gneisenaustraße

A small but interesting selection
of secondhand science fiction and
fantasy where you can hunt for your
favorite books.

SATORI-RECORDS

Wrangelstraße 64
030 531 420 51
werner.holtkamp@tele2.de
www.satori-records.de
Mon-Fri 14:00-19:00; Sat 12:00-16:00
U1 Schlesisches Tor

Secondhand jazz records, art books,
modern paintings, Rosenthal porcelain
and rare wine. Is there anything more
you need to create your perfect Sunday
afternoon atmosphere? At Satori-Records
you can also find chansons and some
unique Sun Ra Disco 3000. Shhh!

PIATTO FORTE

Schlesische Straße 38a
017 011 614 81
baroxmix@gmail.com
www.piattoforteberlin.com
Mon-Fri 12:00-20:00; Sat 12:00-17:00
U1 Schlesisches Tor

Michele, an Italian DJ, and two of his artist
friends opened the record store Piatto
Forte. The place soon became a meeting
point for Berliner DJs, hosting music
events once a month. Don't be fooled by
the arrangement of the space, the shop
window can easily be transformed into a
stage. They mostly sell electro.

TAUSENDUNDEIN BUCH

Gneisenaustraße 60
030 691 46 90
tausendundeinbuch@snafu.de
www.zvab.com
Mon-Fri 11:00-19:00; Sat 11:00-14:00
U7 Gneisenaustraße

Literally translated as '1001 books', this secondhand bookshop smells like old books and cigarettes. You will be welcomed in by a friendly, former literature teacher who opened the shop 27 years ago and loves books of quality. "Nowadays anybody can write a book", she sighs. You find mostly true book lovers here.

UMBRAS KURIOSITÄTEN-KABINETT

Graefestraße 18
030 692 678 1
umbra-book@t-online.de
Mon-Fri 14:00-17:00
U8 Schönleinstraße

A curious place indeed. Umbras Kuriositätenkabinett is an antiquarian bookstore that sells rare philosophy and art titles. You will spot the place as soon as you enter the street because of the huge pile of books (looking like an art installation) standing at the entrance—regardless of the weather.

A&V SECOND-BIKE

Petersburger Straße 74
0163 370 276 8
Mon-Fri 10:00-19:00; Sat 10:00-16:00
U5 Frankfurter Tor

The shop offers secondhand bikes together with used bike components completely checked and in good shape costing 60% less than in regular shops.

ANTIQUARIAT IN FRIEDRICHSHAIN

Niederbarnimstraße 13
030 293 504 04
info@antiquariat-in-friedrichshain.de
www.antiquariat-in-friedrichshain.de
Tue-Fri 14:00-18:00; Sat 12:00-18:00
U5 Frankfurter Tor

A place for scientific books, also available through their online store: www.thomashaker.de. In addition, they carry catalogues in art and architecture. It has a rarified atmosphere and you can find a corner to read in if you wish to.

ANTIQUARIAT MATTHIAS WAGNER

Wühlischstraße 22|23
030 293 517 53
info@antiquariat-wagner.de
www.antiquariat-wagner.de
Mon-Fri 15:00-19:00
U1&S Warschauer Straße

An antiquarian bookstore that also has an online store: www.justbooks.de. It all arose from a love of literature and the wish to be independent. Matthias Wagner sells classic titles for reasonable prices.

ANTIQUARIAT WEIGELT

Proskauerstraße 4
0170 271 6190
antiquariat.weigelt@gmail.com
Wed-Fri 16:00-20:00; Sat 14:00-18:00
U5 Samariterstraße

Run by an ex-professor of literature who is writing a screenplay for a TV show – sounded like something between *Fraser* and *Seinfeld* – and has decided to sell books. I liked the freshness of the cool titles in this antiquarian shop offered alongside rare volumes of fashion catalogues, old *New Yorker* editions and secondhand art books! Fun to see the eclectic mix of old books together with Penguin editions, philosophy, history, music and literature. Good plan B professor!

AUDIO-IN

Libauer Straße 19
030 486 229 4
info@audio-in.net/
www.myspace.com/_audio_in
Mon-Fri 14:00-20:00; Sat 12:00-18:00
S+U1 Warschauer Straße

A used-record store that carries music from the last 30-40 years, specializing in Detroit techno and house, dubstep and electro. This place is also a social meeting point for music lovers and as the records come from all over the world, so do their clients. DJs and collectors appreciate its focus especially here in Berlin where the music scene is predominantly techno. A few names? Casual relief, Planet E, Underground Resistance. Of course, some other genres are also available but don't represent the core business: disco Italo, 80s and 90s dance, and hip hop.

Audio-In spends a lot of time repairing damaged covers and cleaning the records. That's something you will notice immediately.

O-TON RECORDSTORE

Krossener Straße 18
030 293 694 44
Mon-Sat 13:00-20:00
U1+S Warschauer Straße

Although the owner is passionate about 70s rock, he has slowly changed the type of music he sell s to focus on jazz. Still, world music CDs and Eastern European and GDR rock vinyls can also be found on his shelves. Carefully selected, the records look as good as new.

SECOND-BIKE UND SOUND CAFÉ AN & VERKAUF

Warschauer Straße 12
0163 799 579 3
Mon-Sat 10:00-22:00
S+U1 Warschauer Straße

What do bikes have to do with musical instruments? Apparently nothing, but if you are passionate about both you must visit this shop in Friedrichshain. Mountain bikes, cruisers, and racing bikes hang next to guitars, keyboards and amplifiers.

SPARBUCH

Finowstraße 5
030 290 078 93
Wed-Fri 19:00-20:00
U5 Samariter Straße

Looking like a warehouse, this shop sells any type of book for only €1. And if you to want to get rid of your books, they will come and pick them up from your location for free. The condition: don't expect money in return.

BIBLIOTHECA CULINARIA

Zehdenicker Straße 16
030 47 37 75 70
info@ bibliotheca-culinaria.de
www.bibliotheca-culinaria.de
Tue-Fri 11:00-19:00, Sat 11:00-16:00
U8 Rosenthaler Platz

If you are a cooking aficionado, you will be astonished by the diversity and range of cookbooks Bibliotheca Culinaria has to offer. More than just showing practical ways to put ingredients together, this shop of antique cookbooks provides information about the history and lifestyles of the past: books written for American women living in Berlin during World War II that give hints and tips on how to cook German ingredients in an American style, handwritten notebooks of recipes from 1700, Dr. Oetker's recipes for the blind or the editions of Henriette Davidis – the most famous German classic cookbook author, the equivalent of Mrs. Beeton. Add to this, complete annual editions of "Ratgeber für Haus und Familie", cooking with or for children, English and French cookbooks, DDR typical meals, books about cocktails and wine, cooking diet food or for your loved one. Mouth-watering!

BÖTZOW RAD BERLIN

Pasteurstraße 31
030 779 009 40
info@boetzowrad.de/ www.boetzowrad.de
Mon-Fri 10:00-19:00; Sat 10:00-16:00
€M10 Kniprodestraße/Danziger Straße

A women's bikes heaven! Bötzow Rad Berlin sells bikes from the 50s and 70s, mostly Roland (a quality bike brand from Texas), Union and Gazelle. As usual, there is a repair shop attached and after five service visits you get a €5 coupon.

FREAK OUT RECORDS

Prenzlauer Allee 49
030 44 276 15
freakout@snafu.de
Mon-Fri 11:00-19:30; Sat 11:00-16:00
U2 Eberswalder Straße

Opened 21 years ago, Freak Out Records is mixed in terms of style, offering all genres of music in vinyl and CD. It has a particularly wide range of krautrock, garage music and gothic industrial.

MELTING POINT

Kastanienallee 55
030 440 471 31
www.meltingpoint-berlin.de
Mon-Sat 12:00-20:00
U8 Rosenthaler Platz

Focusing heavily on disco, but with techno, jazz and funk also part of the mix. Mitch entered the secondhand record store business 16 years ago and he is also a DJ: "Vinyls are fundamental, I am addicted to them. Imagine, could you ever download and touch such a beautiful cover? It is simply nice to hold it in your hand, put the record on and then see where the needle is going. Music shouldn't be about efficiency, but about enjoying listening to those songs that are on a record". In addition to buying secondhand records from this passionate man, he offers you the chance to test them on one of the record players available in the store.

MOGWA

Prenzlauer Allee 224
030 440 385 65
post@mogwa.de/ www.mogwa.de
Mon-Fri 10:00-19:00; Sat 10:00-16:00
U2 Senefelderplatz

A friendly bookstore with a humanities and literature emphasis.

MUSIKINSTRUMENTE &DESIGN

Schönhauser Allee 28
030 440 336 23
vintageaudioberlin@online.de
www.vintageaudioberlin.de
Mon-Fri 13:30-18:30; closed Thu
U2 Senefelderplatz

Old and antique musical instruments, electronics, vintage equipment, curiosities and rarities from Europe. Lots of guitars hang from the ceiling, trumpets, violins, old microphones, amplifiers, keyboards and analog synthesizers sit around waiting to be played. Are you wondering why old instruments are better than new ones? It's about the skill of the artisan who crafted the instrument and the materials used. Nothing here is younger than 30 years old, and you can go home with a good guitar starting with €60.

RE-CYCLE

Husemannstraße 33
030 921 285 95
Mon-Fri 11:00-20:00; Sat 11:00-18:00
U2 Eberswalder Straße

This small workshop has only a few secondhand bikes each week, but it is worth a try if you're in the neighborhood. You might find exactly what you were looking for.

SAINT GEORGE'S

Wörtherstraße 27
030 817 983 33
info@saintgeorgesbookshop.com
www.saintgeorgesbookshop.com
Mon-Fri 11:00-20:00; Sat 11:00-19:00
U2 Senefelderplatz

The story goes like this: Paul wanted to help a friend of his who had just dropped out of college in London, so he invested money in his London bookstore. Unfortunately, the business failed and he was left with tons of books. Moving to Berlin and opening Saint George's in 2003 just seemed like one of those natural decisions. Selling mostly used but also new books, this place is stocked with interesting titles from London, the only criteria being that the books are in good condition. They support independent publishing houses and hold a monthly experimental literature reading with various writers on Skype. Also, every first Wednesday of the month they organize a 'speak easy', an event where people come and read a passage from a book they like, no matter what language it is in. Cool!

ST. PRENZL'BERG

Schönhauser Allee 41
0160 103 758 1
www.bikepiraten-berlin.de
Mon-Fri 10:30-20:00
U2 Eberswalder Straße

They call themselves the bike pirates and contrary to what you would expect from pirates, the secondhand bikes they sell look loved and taken care of. A large number of used bicycles, all the types you could wish for, sold with a one-year warranty. The shop has a repair service so they also sell used parts.

SCHÖNHAUSER MUSIC I

Schönhauser Allee 70
030 498 093 20
Mon-Sat 11:00-20:00
U2 Eberswalder Straße

A big selection of secondhand CDs, film DVDs and vinyls of nearly all music genres from rock and pop to jazz.

SHAKESPEARE AND SONS

Raumerstraße 36
030 400 036 85
info@shakesbooks.de/ www.shakesbooks.de
Mon-Sat 11:00-19:00
U2 Eberswalder Straße

Coming from Prague where there is a similar bookshop, the owners decided to open a sister Shakespeare and Sons store in Berlin. And as the city has the right number of people speaking English, Spanish and French walking around the streets, they made a wise decision. The space is very inviting, offering comfortable armchairs where you can sit and read. A place to feed your mind and spirit; a place to relax.

SOZIALER BUCHERLADEN

Winsstraße 30
030 884 930 08
Mon-Fri 10:00-17:00; Tue 10:00-19:00
M 10 Winsstraße

The business model here is simple. The books are all donated. You take a book and pay as much as you want to for it and they help immigrants coming from Russia, Georgia or Armenia to find somewhere to live in Germany. This payment method reminds me of my favourite place for home-style cooking: Weinerei on Veteranenstraße 14. Every evening after 20:00 you pay €2 for a glass of wine and help yourself to the delicious food set out on the buffet, then decide how much more you want to pay before you go.

THE RECORDSTORE

Brunnenstraße 186
030 284 446 80
j.adeoshun@hotmail.de
Mon-Sat 12:00-20:00
U8 Rosenthaler Platz

Torsten's record store is a place with a magical aura; it is simply really nice to come here. The shelves offer exclusive titles which are hard to find in Germany like The Sonics, The Beatles and other big names from the 60s, jazz and soul. The new collection focuses on rock'n'roll and indie exclusively.

And talk about glam...the manager of the White Stripes, the Arctic Monkeys, Franz Ferdinand, The Fuzz Tones and Interpol have all stepped in the door to check the place out. You might be lucky and witness an in-store gig with a famous band. In any case, it is just a cool place to hang out.

The Recordstore is also Bassy Club's official record store, a vinyl-only cool club playing "wild music before 1969" as they state on their website.

SOFORTBILD SHOP BERLIN

Brunnestraße 195
030 939 553 42
berlin@sofortbild-shop.de
www.sofortbild-shop.de
Mon-Fri 12:00-20:00; Sat 12:00-18:00
U8 Rosenthaler Platz

If you wonder why Polaroid photography is still so popular in the digital age, the answer is very simple: It's because you get an instant picture. You not only see it, but can hold it and share it with the people around you without having to sign in to a website. But let's face it, it's also part of the vintage trend. Berliners nostalgic for this type of camera are spoiled by having the only shop in Germany selling original Polaroid cameras, Impossible Lift and Fuji films.

The public is wider than you might think. There's an 11 year old who calls in every day to ask for things, a young man traveling to Africa who stocks up on film to take with him, and an 89 year old lady who just takes pictures of the flowers on her balcony. The Polaroid-loving community is always finding new ways to use Polaroid pictures: Impossible Lift is an emulsion that allows you to peel apart the film, modify it and transfer the visual to other surfaces. One smart person has started creating instant Polaroid body tattoos with it. I am telling you, there's a world to explore and SofortBild Shop is planning to organize Polaroid-related workshops soon. Stay Tuned!

'I love the atmosphere of my record store,
the smell of record covers and their design.
This shop is my life.'

TORSTEN, THE RECORDSTORE

The Recordstore

Torsten was disappointed that the music industry were pushing CDs and forgetting about the quality of the music played on vinyls, so he wanted to fight the current trend and promote the better sound and soul of records by opening a store. He started by selling a few private collections from Texas and the UK: "It was easy because records are so special and I opened this shop for a collector's soul". Now he finds that people are interested in vinyls in a specific part of their life, at the age of 20 and not 40 like one would expect. I guess it's also the fact that Berlin offers a coolness factor to all those interested in retro, vintage and secondhand.

Torsten's opinion is that mp3s don't make you feel in touch with the music and the proof that this music medium is getting less interesting is that some new vinyls come with a free CD attached or with a download code. Things have turned the other way around for a bit.

"I love the atmosphere of my record store, the smell of record covers and their design. This shop is my life", says Torsten - an original Prenzlauer Berger.

UNTERWEGS

Torstraße 93
030 440 560 15
unterwegs@berlinbook.com
www.berlinbook.com
Tue-Fri 15:00-19:00; Sat 12:00-15:00
U8 Rosenthaler Platz

Is it a photo gallery? Is it an art space? Or a new bookstore? None of the above. It is a secondhand and antiquarian bookstore. Marie Luise Surek-Becker has made the shop look sleek and fancy to reflect the area and the people living close by. Books as well as original photography and portfolios with a focus on architecture and Berlin are spread on spacious shelves. But the highlights are the travel guides, Baedeker and Meyer from 1827 up to 1945. She is among the few in the world selling them. Some are very old and very rare, some not and so their price ranges from €10 and €10,000. Either way, this is a place with something for every budget. If you have a special request, you will be put on a list and contacted when the item is found. If you are among the steady customers, you'll get a catalogue with listings on a regular basis. That's pretty cool!

BUCH UND KUNSTANTIQUARIAT TODE

Dudenstraße 36
030 786 518 6
antiquariattode@t-online.de
Mon-Fri 13:00-20:00; Sat 12:00-16:00
U6 Platz der Luftbrücke

The books here are so interesting that clients actually want to spend the night in the store. Opened in 1973, the shop sells mainly works of literature dating back to 1600 (some signed by the authors), but also philosophy, history and natural science. Check out the integrated small art gallery with paintings and sketches in the back.

DEUKER PIANOS&FLÜGEL

Dudenstraße 36
030 786 471 9
deukerpiano@t-online.de
www.deukerpiano.de
Wed-Fri 12:00-18:00; Sat 10:00-14:00
U6 Platz der Luftbrücke

Kembel, Yamaha and other brands of new and used pianos. Martin Deuker, a piano technician himself, offers repair services as well as renting pianos for private events.

GAMES & HANDYS. ANKAUF VERKAUF TAUSCH

Kolonnenstraße 66
030 966 142 23
Mon-Fri 10:00-20:00; Sat 11:00-19:00
U7 Kleistpark

Game addicts, here is something for you: secondhand game DVDs, Nintendo DS cards, PSP, Kinect, X Box and mobile accessories for €15-25. If you have already played one of your games many times or are just bored with it, you can trade it in here for a new one.

ASA90

Fuldastraße 55
030 623 100 1
mail@asa90.com/ asa90.com
Tue-Fri 11:00-19:00; Sat 11:00-16:00
U7 Rathaus Neukölln

This 100 year-old shop sells vintage and
secondhand cameras from 1910 and later.
There are just a few digital cameras and
only by chance. Analog and film are the
words of the day. And you get a six-month
warranty for any purchased product.
"The camera has to fit the person and
their goals and I always advise of the
best and cheapest option", says the
owner of ASA90. Some of the real stars
of the collection are the flashes, the
60mm projectors and the developing
and scanning lab in the back.

BUCHLADEN BUNBURY

Weserstraße 210
030 680 808 04
Mon-Fri 11:00-20:00; Sat 11:00-19:00
U8 Hermannplatz

With a friendly host and a cosy atmosphere, Bunbury has one of the best selections of literature around.

CITY RAD

Richardstraße 112
030 531 490 38
Mon-Fri 10:00-20:00; Sat 10:00-14:00
U7 Karl-Marx-Straße

Some of the nicest vintage bikes await you inside this store. Large both in size and number of choices, you can find bikes to match any age or gender.

DIE BIOGRAFISCHE BIBLIOTHEK

Richardstraße 55
030 680 593 87
biobib@online.de/ www.biobib.info
Mon-Fri 15:00-19:00; closed Wed
U7 Neukölln

Taking a peek at people's intimate lives has always been something of an interest. And the selection of biographies, memoires and letters contained in this shop are a good tool for doing just that. Owned by an ex-teacher, the shop is connected to the art space next door where on the last Friday of every month a reading takes place.

FAHRRAD UND MOPEDLADEN

Pflügerstraße 75
030 534 700 9
Mon-Fri 9:00-18:00; Sat 9:00-12:00
U8 Schönleinstraße

The real Berlin hipster is a vintage lover and owns a Simson Schwalbe moped. Produced in the GDR, Simson motorcycles ceased being made in the 1960s because of a government decision, but they remain forever in the hearts of nostalgics. Whether you are looking to buy one or just repair yours, you can't find a better place than Fahrrad und Mopeladen where these mopeds are treated like royalty. Besides being beautiful, Schwalbe are the fastest way to travel on two wheels. Prices start from €500 and go up to €1500.

FITS

Weichselstraße 59
030 544 620 69
smile@fitsberlin.de / www.fitsberlin.de
Tue-Sat 13:00-20:00
U7 Rathaus Neukölln

A haven where bikes that have been left to rust in the back of a garage are rescued and restored, ready to find a new owner. That's what Jeroen van Hofwegen and Lena Maierhof do at FITS, their newly opened second-hand racing bike shop. The shop, located in their comfy house on the ground floor of a building in Neukölln, is like a dream come true as they are totally in love with racing bikes. You can even repair your own bike at their place, they will hand you the right tools. They can't wait to meet you.

> ## 'I was so in love with racing bikes and many of my friends actually wanted to own one.'

JEROEN VAN HOFWEGEN, FITS

FITS

Jeroen van Hofwegen and Lena Maierhof opened FITS in the front room of their apartment in Neukölln. A graphic designer and a skateboarding fan, Jeroen comes from the Netherlands. Lena describes the store as being a 'klein traum' (a little dream) of hers. The idea came up after finishing her cultural science studies and it was the result of balancing her passion for racing bikes and against the need for money: "I was so in love with racing bikes and many of my friends actually wanted to own one."

But Lena not only admires the bikes from distance, but also repairs, checks and cleans them. "I worked in a bike shop for an entire summer. At the beginning it was a bit nasty but I enjoyed learning and working with the parts that make up these special bikes. Moreover, I now know a lot of tips and tricks for repairing bikes". That's how FITS makes all their bikes prettier and fully functional. They don't earn their living with this business, but instead they put a lot of love and good thoughts in making people happier with a vintage racing bike. For them it's fun and that's enough.

GLÜCKSVELO

Pannierstraße 53a
0178 745 514 5
info@gluecksvelo.de / www.gluecksvelo.de
Tue-Fri 9:00-12:00, 14:00-19:00;
Sat 11:00-16:00
U8 Hermannplatz

GlücksVelo is a mecca for racing bikes. The young duo who run the place dedicate time to advising clients either on taking care of their old bikes or on finding the appropriate used bike. The bikes come from France and Southern Italy.

HOME & INTERIORS

Furniture / Lighting
Appliances / Electronics
Homewares

WHEN YOU THINK OF FURNITURE IN GERMANY, MANY EUROPEANS WOULD THINK OF BAUHAUS. AND THAT IS APPROPRIATE. CONSIDERED OLD FASHIONED IN POST-WAR TIMES, SINCE THE 1990S BAUHAUS DESIGN HAS BEEN CONSIDERED TRENDY AND SOUGHT AFTER AND IS NOW MAKING WAVES IN BERLIN'S VINTAGE FURNITURE SHOPS.

Other modern designs and names like Charles Eames or Christian Dell are also desirable and make up the high-end vintage home and interiors scene. Apart from that, charming designs from unknown names can be found in plenty of shops and sometimes even lying on the sidewalk, waiting for somebody to appreciate them (take a walk on Urbanstraße in Kreuzberg starting from Hermannplatz and you will see what I mean).

If I were to choose between types of furniture, I'd say kitchen cabinets are a specialty in Berlin-- massive pieces that come in a variety of pale hues and offer a peek into the intimacy of tableware. There is something romantic attached to them that fits so well into Berlin's breakfast culture.

But home is not only about furniture. People also need lamps and, surprisingly or not, industrial lamps are fashionable in Berlin at the moment. When I say industrial, I mean literally industrial pieces taken from soon-to-be demolished plants and warehouses and bought for kitchens or dining rooms.

The popularity of vintage has influenced not only people's behavior, but also the market and the number of shops. Suarezstraße in Charlottenburg hosts around 20 antiques and vintage stores right next to each other, therefore the street has been called the Berliner Antiques Street (some but not all of its stores are featured in the book). Since glossy magazines started introducing secondhand furniture or revivals of classic designs into their editorials, many have decided to start mixing the new with the old inside their homes.

In addition, we have sourced all sorts of electronic appliances, recycled designs and anything else you might place inside your house to make it look more cosy or more crazy. This last characteristic is achieved in mash-ups. They are what we call all-in-one shops, with everything you need--and don't need-- for your home.

Let's see where we find all this...

ADLER ANTIK

Urbanstraße 124
030 695 376 87
Mon-Fri 10:00-19:00; Sat 10:00-17:00
U8 Schönleinstraße

In this typical secondhand furniture store, owned by Turkish brothers, you can get high quality at a good price. Many chairs, massive cupboards and living room furniture appropriate for those who have spacious rooms. The pieces are piled up inside the store, but the hosts are friendly and will help you with anything you need. The oldest piece they had at the time of my arrival: a cabinet from 1890.

KLASSIKERFUNDUS

Südstern 6
030 644 906 00
mail@klassikerfundus.de/klassikerfundus.de
Tue-Fri 12:00-19:00; Sat 12:00-16:00
U7 Südstern

What in 1903 was a car shop is now a space with authentic industrial architecture. The basement of Klassikerfundus offers factory lamps and lots of vintage desk lamps: imagine lamps of all types lined up in a room with the unfinished grey stone walls. You are in the spotlight, in the focus of huge vintage film and photography lights. The producers of *Inglourious Basterds* rented one of them. Not to be missed!

GUERILLIAZ

Gneisenaustraße 55
0178 53 04 996
nora-krauss@gmx.de / www.guerilliaz.de
Mon-Fri 11:00-19:00; Sat 11:00-16:00
U7 Südstern

Guerilliaz is a place you might just want to move into because its interior is so appealing. Full of charm and character, this store and workshop sells revived objects: old window frames that now display jewellery, repainted wooden hangers and so on. Sometimes the owners find interesting pieces of furniture abandoned on the sidewalk and offer them a new aesthetic, life and purpose. The furniture becomes a collage of times and lives.

KOMFORT 36

Schlesische Straße 38a
030 616 207 81
komfort36@gmx.de / www.komfort36.com
Thu-Fri 14:00-19:30; Sat 13:00-18:00
U1 Schlesisches Tor

Well-displayed Braun, Bauhaus, Danish, Scandinavian, Italian and German designs: Egon Eiermann, Wilhelm Wagenfeld, Børge Mogensen, Gino Sarfatti and Kartell are some of the names you will find in this strikingly beautiful shop. A trend in interior design, according to the owner, is that it's all about modern classic mixed with antique pieces. A while ago, people were crazy about 70s furniture, now they are into 50s industrial design and then there are the all time classics like Bauhaus, Christian Dell, Le Corbusier and Charles Eames. You will find all of these in this charming showroom in East Berlin, objects that are no longer being produced. This one is for collectors.

KRAMARI

Gneisnaustraße 91
030 613 041 27
kramari@kramari.de / www.kramari.de
Tue-Fri 14:00-19:00; Sat 12:00-17:00
U7 Gneisenaustraße

Nina Hagen and Michael Stipe from R.E.M. purchased their lamps from Kramari. Owned by an architect and his wife, the 50s and 60s lighting store was opened in 2003. Both super-brands and everyday lamps are to be found in this friendly space. Vintage icons spotted: an old Saber radio and Colombos light globes.

NESTHOCKER

Graefestraße 75
030 690 046 97
mail@nesthocker-berlin.de
www.nesthocker-berlin.de
Tue-Fri 14:00-19:00; Sat 12:00-15:00
U8 Schönleinstraße

Remember the creaky sound old wooden floorboards make when you walk on them? That's how Nesthocker feels. But the content is far from being unpretentious. The store immediately takes your breath away: furniture collected from France, England or brought by the owner's (a part-time doctor) friends. Tall geographical maps from a school near Frankfurt and drawings of biological subjects go together with shabby chic furniture, industrial design, art deco bags and chairs picked up from a farm. Clearly the selection is mediated by a taste-maker.

POLSTEREI & GALERIE

Graefestraße 90
030 666 551 65
info@polstereinowel.de
www.polstereinowel.de
Mon-Fri 10:00-18:00; Sat 11:00-16:00
U8 Schönleinstraße

Can we call old designs on new materials – 'authentic' recycling? This upholstery workshop, located on one of the busiest streets of Graefekiez, appealed to me with its Art Nouveau and Art Deco textile designs. The store plus workshop has been refurbishing vintage furniture and bringing it back to life in an authentic manner, for the last 25 years. At the time of my visit, work on a majestic couch from the American 1920s was about to be completed after 200 hours. The cost? €13,000.

PONY HÜTCHEN

Pücklerstraße 33
030 698 186 79
lilli@pretty-stuff.de/ www.pretty-stuff.de
Mon-Sat 15:00-20:00
U1 Görlitzer Bahnhof

Friendly prices, furniture that you instantly want to buy, plus clothes and happiness. That's what Pony Hütchen claims to sell. The shop is always packed with items that are randomly displayed, but it is like being on a treasure hunt. It's full of quirky and charming things.

SCHUBLADEN

Körtestraße 26
030 616 511 49
mail@schubladen.de/ www.schubladen.de
Tue-Fri 11:00-19:00; Sat 11:00-16:00
U7 Südstern

Schubladen sure knows how to bring in a twist of vintage and inject a story into a piece of furniture. Whether it is a cupboard, a wardrobe or a bedside table, Schubladen equips them with vintage, one-off, left over drawers. The layers of patina are left intact, but the dirt that has built up over time is removed so they can be fully functional yet still keep their history. In their previous lives, the drawers might have been used in a car workshop, a pharmacy or an old lingerie shop. "Sometimes you can read the labels and guess where they come from or what they were for like 'lamp/red'. Once I traced the background of a drawer that was originally from Germany, ended up in an electricity garage in Luxemburg and then came into my hands. I like it when things don't have an immediate value and I place them in a new context so their energy can come back to the surface", says Franziska Wodicka, the brilliant mind behind the concept.

SHÖWRAUM

Schönleinstraße 3
030 488 135 88
mail@showraum.de/ www.showraum.de
open from morning to late evening, but call
for an appointment
U8 Schönleinstraße

I have passed by this place a hundred times and was always curious about what was inside. The outside looked like a cross between an art gallery and an Italian bakery, but I was never there during their opening times. One day, I stopped in front to admire the shop window again and a guy on a bike stopped and said "I have the key, do you want to come in?" A world of handmade furniture and product design created from used and found materials opened in front of my eyes. I knew it! I knew this place was hiding something wonderful. It's high-end recycled design... first you fall in love with the object and then you realize it was something else in its past life. Perhaps a piece of tire, an unwanted couch, a floorboard or a mere piece of metal. The guys at ShöwRaum give it a life of its own, an industrial, masculine look and sell it as affordable art.

ShöwRaum

Meet the ShöwRaum gang! Jaap Wijnants studied art in Holland and owned a bike company that he decided to sell because he 'missed making stuff', Patrick Kerti is a furniture designer and just happened to rent a desk in this space where he met and married Regitze Kerti who is actually the founder of the place – a Danish architect - and Sebastian Mall is the carpenter - just came in for a project and decided to stay. It all started as an office space, but what they really wanted to do is to incorporate recycling and design into high-end furniture made of quality materials. "We wanted people first to see and like what they see and then realize what it is actually made of", says Jaap.

If the design is not high end, these pieces end up in the garbage bin and ShöwRaum gives them a proper makeover. They find the materials on the street and just recently started also to buy them from various places like demolition companies.

These guys definitely sell affordable art and aspire to working together on big projects like refurbishing hotels. They have an idealistic view, far from the industrial process and after they sell one of their hand crafted pieces, they miss it. They enjoy one-to-one creation and so people spend money and sometimes even co-create with the team, on something made only for them. A true love for craft!

"We are romantic and appreciate aesthetics. We are not looking to build technologically innovative pieces. We like textiles, the uniqueness of a found object on the street and we're working to recover its beauty", states Patrick.

'We wanted people first to see and like what they see and then realize what it is actually made of'

JAAP, SHÖWRAUM

A&V WASCHBÄR

Kopernikusstraße 12
030 297 728 44
technik@auv-waschbaer.de
www.auv-waschbaer.de
Mon-Fri 10:00–19:00; Sat 10:00-16:00
U1&S Warschauer Straße

Waschbär is about washing machines,
dryers, dishwashers, freezers and fridges
plus home entertainment devices. If you
have an extra appliance at home that you
wish to sell through them, they will come
and pick it up for free.

KUNST UND ANTIQUITÄTEN

Schreinerstraße 64a
030 426 681 816
r.petter@petter-antiquitaeten.de
www.petter-antiquitaeten.com
Mon-Fri; Sat:
U5 Samariterstraße

Collectors for more than 25 years, Gabi
and Rainer Petter chose to focus their
antique and secondhand offerings on rare
porcelain, antique furniture, paintings
and bronze statuettes.

GRÜNBERGER AN & VERKAUF

Grünberger Straße 44
030 290 491 47
Mon-Fri 10:00-19:00; Sat 10:00-17:00
U5 Frankfurter Tor

Don't be fooled by the heaps of
secondhand jewellery lying on a dining
table in the front of this store's entrance.
This Grünberger secondhand store is
mainly about lamps, art and furniture
from any decade, some of it is rare and
some not so rare. You'll be intrigued.

ORIGINAL IN BERLIN

Karl-Marx-Allee 94
030 609 360 46
lars@originalinberlin.de
www.originalinberlin.de
Mon-Fri 11:00-19:00; Sat 12:00-16:00
U5 Weberwiese

Lars, the driving force behind Original in Berlin is a very passionate vintage soul and his enthusiasm is catching. To make a long story short, at 20 he started to buy Panton chairs, played drums in a band and listened to lots of 60s music, bought a 60s car and last, but not least, got interested in space age furniture in order to give his vintage life a holistic approach. His taste evolved to American mid-century modern and this is the focus of his shop today. He buys many of the pieces in America such as Herman Miller, Eames, Paul McCobb, Marshall Studios, adding that when it comes to the criteria for selection: "My taste is my direction".

Original in Berlin has its own upholsterers and carpenters so they can tailor things to your request. "I don't like the gallery look of vintage furniture shops. I would like to make it look more like a workshop, a place where you can get the handcrafted feeling".

Working together with international auction houses like Phillips de Pury, Wright20, and Christie's, they have access to old stock and items in big quantities (lamps of a specific design or Eames shelves for example) so, they could actually furnish big spaces like restaurants.

PIRA X - BERLIN

Niederbarnimstraße 20
0177 154 318 1
schmale-berlin@t-online.de
Mon, Tue, Fri, Sat 14:00-20:00
U5 Samariterstraße

Pira-X comes in with a lot of charm and a strong feminine character. Furniture, lamps and accessories from the 20s to 70s are harmoniously displayed making you want to wander around for hours to investigate every corner. Chic and retro!

TECHNISCHER AN & VERKAUF

Frankfurter Allee 68
030 212 375 85
Mon-Fri 10-18; Sat 10:00-14:00
U5 Samariterstraße

The shop, which has been around for 20 years, offers very good quality secondhand electronics. It carries a large range of electronic items such as computer monitors, TVs, DVD players, amplifiers, stereos, as well as being a Playstation and Nintendos paradise. You also get a warranty of from three months up to one year depending on the item. And if the Game Boy was part of your childhood, you definitely have a strong reason to go there.

A&V TECH

Eberswalder Straße 29
030 440 496 10
sadik21@hotmail.de
Mon-Fri 11:00-19:00; Sat 12:00-20:00
U2 Eberswalder Straße

Piled up to the ceiling, leaving just a thin corridor to walk between them: computers, washing machines, fridges, TVs, game console and other hi-fi stuff.

DER MÖBELLADEN

Wörther Straße 15
030 440 375 60
mail@der-moebelladen-berlin.de
www.dermoebelladen-berlin.de
Tue-Fri 12:00-19:00; Sat 11:00-16:00
U2 Senefelderplatz

The curator here, Jenno Fulde, has a background in German studies and theater, but earns his money by selling refurbished baroque furniture. Emphasizing the usability of the items, he says he is not selling art pieces but furniture in the style of Gründerzeit, Biedermeier and Art Nouveau. Although my attention was grabbed by the industrial look of an operating table, it's only there by chance. He normally sells large wooden tables that are made from the old floorboards of the flats around in Berg.

E-HAUS

Schliemannstraße 1
030 488 260 44
zahirhajjo@yahoo.de
Mon-Sat 10:00-20:00
U2 Eberswalder Straße

Geared up with lots of electronic
appliances and brands like Siemens,
Philips, Miele, Braun and Bosch, E-Haus
offers a 12-month warranty on any
product. Delivery and repair are
also available.

FRIEDRICHS LUST SCHREIBER +MOZEDLANI

Schönhauser Allee 8
030 517 362 56
info@ friedrichslust.de / friedrichslust.de
Thu-Fri 15:00-19:00; Sat 12:00-18:00
U2 Rosa-Luxemburg-Platz

Collecting is almost part of being human
and something that very few people
manage to live without. Fewer manage
to offer their collections outside their
own home. Schreiber +Mozedlani did and
in their shop you will find extravagant
art pieces, antiquities, decorations and
restored furniture but also less popular
objects like gymnastics equipment from
1900 that can be rented. They share their
restored pieces or their own creations
with shoots for magazines, films and TV
productions. "We love finding old things,
we look for the extravagant and we are
happy when we can sell it to cool people",
say the owners.

> '*Berlin has a big vintage shops scene and we can all co-exist*'
>
> **JULIANA, MÖBEL KOMBINAT**

Möbel&Stiefel Kombinat

Juliana's father worked for years in the apartment clearance business so, from the time she was young, she often accompanied her father when he was picking-up and distributing the merchandise to various stores. That's how she developed a taste for old things and vintage: "I was happy to see so many people going crazy for old furniture when I was with my dad visiting his friends' shops like VEB Orange and so I became aware of these items."

Later she became a dental assistant but the job didn't pay enough money, so she turned to her childhood experience and opened a secondhand boots store in Oderberger Straße using her father's expertise and contacts to get off to a good start. The business grew very fast and she continued talking to her clients asking them what other secondhand items they wanted. There were two big requests that resulted in two new shops: men's clothing (the store on Eberswalder Straße) and

later on, furniture (Möbel Kombinat). "Men used to wear clothes until they wore out so it is harder to find men's wearables and they are, of course, more expensive than women's clothing", says Juliana.

Juliana has an interesting observation regarding competition in the secondhand market, saying it barely exists: "Almost all the items are unique, so I also advise people to go to look for what they wish for in other shops. Berlin has a big vintage shops scene and we can all co-exist". There are still many attics and cellars that are filled with things from the GDR times and now they need to be emptied. That's where businesses like Juliana's come into the game and can profit.

Her prediction for the future is quite harsh however, "secondhand will die because the quality of the upcoming decades is getting lower and lower. Textiles barely last for a year, so they can't survive until the next decade."

KOLLWITZ KABINETT

Wörtherstraße 31
030 218 012 32
kollwitzkabinett@web.de
Mon-Fri 13:00–19:00; Sat 11:00-17:00
U2 Eberswalder Straße

Käthe Kollwitz was a beloved German painter and sculptor who showed her empathy for the poor, the hungry and victims of war through her work. The attraction of this shop that brings her to mind is the extensive collection of art: paintings, lithographs and other artistic items from the Expressionist and Art Deco periods brought here straight from the auction houses. Shiny chandeliers from Austria give a ballroom feeling to the entire space, and the frames of the paintings are sourced at flea markets so they can match the time period of the painting itself. The style suits the houses in the area, and as Eva, the owner, says, "the boundary between art and kitsch is very thin, but there is always the need for a drop of it". That's probably why she also sells decorative sculptures. Do drop by, she likes to meet people who share her tastes.

KUNST-A-BUNT

Wörther Straße 39
030 443 577 35
info@kunst-a-bunt.de/ www.kunst-a-bunt.de
Mon-Fri 11:00-19:00; Sat 11:00-17:00
U2 Senefelderplatz

Wine from the Rhine region, books, lamps and lots of paintings arranged as if in a gallery, sit together with porcelain sets and ceramics. Once a year this place really turns into a gallery and hosts the work of artists from the neighbourhood.

LAMPENMANUFAKTUR BERLIN

Rykestraße 51
030 440 451 32
info@lampenmanufaktur-berlin.de
www.lampenmanufaktur-berlin.de
Mon-Fri 12:00–19:00; Sat 10:00-18:00
U2 Eberswalder Straße

Copies of antique lamps are created every day with components from Italy, Poland and sometimes from Turkey. Originals also end up here after apartment clearances and Lampenmanufaktur revives them. They are mostly from the 1920s to 1950s, Art Deco, Art Nouveau, brass lamps and Bauhaus style. What's the big trend in lamps right now? Shhh, don't tell, it's classical design with a technical look. And if you have just bought a lamp from the flea market and realized it doesn't work, they can help you with that too.

MAGASIN

Lychener Straße 3
030 747 725 60
info@magasin-berlin.de
www.magasin-berlin.de
Mon-Fri 14:00–20:00; Sat 12:00-18:00
U2 Eberswalder Straße

The focus is on mid-century modern design. When you come inside you feel the items have space to breathe. This is not one of those secondhand stores where the items are piled up to the ceiling, but a real showroom where each piece of furniture is in the spotlight and receives the right amount of attention. Although you might expect to see named brands here, what you will find is just good quality furniture. The store is tailored to the PrenzlBergers' taste for vintage design, nicely finished.

MÖBEL KOMBINAT BERLIN

Wolliner Straße 18-19
030 754 572 80
info@stiefelkombinat.de
www.stiefelkombinat.de
Mon-Sat 12:00-20:00
U8 Bernauer Straße

Meet the sister shop, the furniture variant, of Stiefelkombinat! The idea of supplementing it with a furniture store came about four years ago after Juliana found out from her regular customers that all they were missing in terms of vintage was cool furniture. So, furniture it is! And now, they can have more of their wishes granted, because Juliana notes down their requests and as soon as she finds the desired items, she calls her clients. Her focus is on 60s to 80s furniture and interior design. My favourite is the original wallpaper from the GDR that comes in many patterns. So chic!

● ● ●

OBJETS TROUVÉS. NONCHALANTES WOHNEN

Rykestraße 32A
0163 181 098 5
ot-berlin@gmx.de
www.objets-trouves-berlin.de
Wed-Sat 12:00–19:00
U2 Eberswalder Straße

Shabby chic or nonchalant living as the headline says, means vintage and un-restored industrial furniture and objects for interiors that are given a new context. You'll fall in love with French industrial pieces, medicine cabinets, file cabinets all found on the streets of Europe where Robert Hohberg and Magdalena Arnold travel. The pieces are then 'sensitively' re-touched or cleaned and made fully functional. There's a mix of 20s-50s classics from Belgium, Holland, Czech Republic and Germany.

● ● ●

STUDIO ZIBEN

Danziger Straße 22
030 347 162 77
info@studio-ziben.de
www.studio-ziben.de
Tue-Sat 12:00-19:00
M10 Husemannstraße

Mariusz Malecki, a Polish designer, is inspired by the city of Berlin to create new designs out of carpenters' waste or by reviving and repurposing pieces of wood he finds abandoned on the streets. The outcome is a remarkable combination of old and new with a lot of feeling and a story to tell. Shelves made of floorboards, glass cabinets that receive old windows as doors, small cabinets and desks made from recycled wood. "I build fairytales", Mariusz says. I agree.

ZWISCHENZEIT

Raumerstraße 35
030 446 733 71
chris@ zwischenzeit.org
www.zwischenzeit.org
Mon-Fri 14:00-19:00
U2 Eberswalder Straße

Let me guess. It's a hot summer night and you're planning a pool party. You need cool looking bowls for lemonade from Italy or France for your garden aperitif, vintage glasses for the cocktails, vases to put the flowers in, vinyls for the jazzy background atmosphere and perhaps also a new coffee table. Everything you are looking for in glassware from the 70s plus some 50s interiors items is here at Zwischenzeit.

AUS ZWEITER HAND

Torstraße 98
030 282 236 7
Mon-Fri 13:00-19:00
U8 Rosenthaler Platz

The shop has a long history and has existed since GDR times. Back then, a secondhand store was the only place where you could buy an item from the West, but now it has been transformed into a place where you can buy special things that are probably (and hopefully) no longer mass-produced. In the time of the GDR, it was a state monopoly and the owner had to sell what the state wanted him to sell which was children's clothes. After the wall fell, he was able to start selling antiques and anything else he wanted. The unexpected element of what will come into his store each day is one of the things that makes his job fun. Miniature trains, toys, porcelain, mobile phones and other electronic stuff.

STUE

Torstraße 70
030 247 276 50
mail@stueberlin.de/ stueberlin.de
Mon-Sat 12:00-19:00
U2 Rosa-Luxemburg-Platz

Owned by a former rock/pop singer who learned how to build guitars, Stue showcases rescued Danish furniture from the 20th century. Heike's interest is in selling refurbished furniture that will be functional and decorate your house for the next 50 years. Their value comes from their usability, handcrafted shapes and patina. As Heike never thinks of the price in terms of how much the piece might be auctioned for, the prices are fair. Contemporary ceramics, jewellery, handbags, porcelain, art and other products are shown and sold along with the vintage pieces. Independent artists sometimes display their creations inside the store so the space occasionally acts like an art gallery.

20TH CENTURY INTERIOR BERLIN

Münzstraße 19 - 1st backyard
030 854 051 41
fahrein@20thcenturyinterior.com
www.20thcenturyinterior.com
Tue-Sat 12:00-18:00 or by appointment
U2 Rosa-Luxemburg-Platz

Here you will learn from Tobias Allan Fahrein how much vintage items can introduce flair and personality to a home. This exclusive vintage furniture showroom harmoniously displays selected pieces, though the deposit room downstairs offers endless possibilities. The items you find here are rare, original and well-loved with a time frame stretching to the 60s. "I find them, or they find me and together they form something between a shop and an art museum", says Tobias.

WAAHNSINN

Rosenthaler Straße 17
030 282 002 9
shop@waahnsinn-berlin.de
www.waahnsinn-berlin.de
Mon-Sat 9:00-18:00
U8 Weinmeisterstraße

This store is packed with a crazy array of things--lamps, 60s cocktail chairs, egg garden chairs, Melitta cups, 50s-70s sunglasses, some items of furniture, things from the GDR period like cups and pots or vintage Playboy magazines, original microphones and retro telephones. Many of the items come from Luxemburg, Holland and Germany. The shop also rents tuxedos and furniture for film and theater and carries a few new lines of clothes from local designers. Don't forget to ask about the cellar!

Stue

Heike, the owner of Stue, was a vocal performer in an indie rock band in the 90s and she still sings now in a band called Metal Ghost, but pregnancy made her decide to consider something more stable and safe. Being half Danish, she found herself on holiday in Denmark where she felt the urge to buy a whole stall of furniture from a flea market because she loved it. In Berlin she had furnished her flat from flea markets, but it would be with heavy pieces that were hard to handle or move around. Danish style was exactly what she needed – light, sleek and stylish – so, she bought the stall, came back to Berlin and opened a shop in Schöneberg. Later on, Prenzlauer Bergers complained she was too far away as most of her clients lived there so now she is on Torstraße, after being chased from the now too expensive Schönhauser Allee. "Here it's still dirty and loud and not really on the way... people who come here know exactly what they want. I like that."

In terms of her clients, she says: "At first they were irritated saying they hated this stuff their parents used to have, but after a while people discovered its merits and got over their prejudices and started appreciating it for what it was: handcrafted and functional". People in Berlin were afraid of settling in because inhabitants of this crazy city want to have a sort of rambling cowboy lifestyle, sleeping on a couch or on a mattress thrown in a corner of the floor that gives this freedom and flexibility. But now, much younger people visit Stue to look for a nice piece of furniture for their flat.

"What I love about my shop is that the objects inside come together in a coherent visual. I somehow manage to match elements and I also do interior design and furnishing for flats. Sometimes I just rearrange things that clients already own, making the best out of what they have for their lives and needs. Thinking about fitting things together resembles how I create music", says Heike.

'What I love about my shop is that the objects inside come together in a coherent visual.'

HEIKE, STUE

ANTIK & MODERNE

Belzigerstraße 24
030 887 192 10
stephan.burda@gmx.de
www.berlinburdawohnungsaufloesungen.de
Mon-Fri 12:00-18:00; Sat 11:00-14:00
U7 Eisenacher Straße

They call it items from your grandparents'
time, but others say it is 70s modern
design furniture. Whatever you call it,
in addition to furniture and chandeliers,
you will find dinnerware services from
Hutschenreuther porcelain and various
objects made of 60s and 70s glass. The
Schöneberg neighborhood has *altbau*
apartments and this store is perfect
for people who wish to decorate
them authentically.

PETERSEN FERNSEHDIENST

Kolonnenstraße 51
030 781 474 7
petersen.fernsehdienst@yahoo.de
www.fernsehdienstpetersen.de
Mon-Fri 10:00-20:00; Sat 10:00-18:00
U7 Kleistpark

Wii consoles, TVs, cables, cassette players,
washing machines, dishwashers, stoves
(with a one-year warranty). Even though
this shop is more expensive than some,
you have the safety of not having to buy
a replacement after two months of use.
Great deals!

RESTPOSTEN AN + VERKAUF

Dudenstraße 32
030 854 086 44
Mon-Fri 10:00-20:00; Sat 11:00-16:00
U6 Platz der Luftbrücke

All electronics, computers, TVs, CDs, mobile phones, refrigerators, music cables, headsets and coffee machines as well as a few bicycles. Even though the shop is a mess, Metin creates a neighborhood feeling, offering cheap and convenient products. While we chatted he greeted every passer-by and offered me a drink of ayran (a popular Turkish yogurt drink). A couple of minutes later, he helped a lady who had just bought a new bike from somewhere to oil her bicycle chain. The shop is also a delivery spot so you can leave your package there and Metin will make sure the delivery person picks it up.

ART+INDUSTRY

Bleibtreustraße 40
030 883 494 6
info@aiberlin.de
www.artindustryberlin.de
Mon-Fri 14:00-18:30; Sat 11:00-16:00
S Savignyplatz

The owner's love of watches and vintage objects started when he spent time looking over his watchmaker father's shoulder as he worked. In his shop now, you can find a vast collection of vintage wristwatches which are accompanied by a one-year warranty, table clocks, 50s and 60s cufflinks (lovely!), rings and bracelets from the USA and France, beautiful 30s Art Deco necklaces and lots of amber jewelry.

The furniture is carefully selected, not by brand, but by tradition and technique. Having close contacts with architects and private collectors, he feels that it is important to know the background of items, about the techniques used and the times when they were produced in order to understand their value.

The main furniture showroom is only a few blocks away on Wilmersdorferstaße, but it is only opened on Tuesdays from 11:00 to 18:00 or by appointment. There you can find more tubular steel furniture, armchairs and sofas, desks, dining tables, cabinets and lamps of the 20s to the 50s. A full restoration service and rental of props is available.

HANS-PETER JOCHUM

Bleibtreustraße 41
030 882 161 2
hpjochum@snafu.de
www.hpjochum.de
Mon-Fri 14:00-18:30; Sat 11:00-16:00
U1 Uhlandstraße

Hans-Peter Jochum is one of the most pleasant and stimulating people on the Berliner vintage scene. In this business for 25 years, he owns a little shop with carefully selected original furniture from the 50s plus a gallery space on Knesebeckstraße 54 that changes its content pretty often. Original, colourful rugs from Morocco accompany the historical design.

He states that "Today vintage furniture is an online business, but we don't do this because we like experiencing the materials and touching them, finding out about things you would not search for. You'd search for Eames but you would not discover new designs". His advice is that we should be free to put things together: a chair from Iraq, a table from Italy and a lamp from America in order to create notable interiors.

L&M LEE

Kurfürstendamm 32
030 881 733 3
info@lampen-lee-berlin.de
www.lampen-lee-berlin.de
Mon-Sat opening at 10:00
U1 Uhlandstraße

In 1972 this was an antique store selling porcelain and jewelry. Now they sell original lamps and replicas from the 1900s to 1930s. As Berlin contains many Art Nouveau apartments, this style fits in perfectly. In addition, they showcase Art Deco jewellery, porcelain and covers, kitchenware, nightgowns, aprons and shirts from 1910. Its long history makes it popular with VIPs and TV stars. I even heard that Bob Dylan stopped in right before the wall fell. Expensive but classy.

REISEANTIQUITÄTEN

Suarezstraße 48-49
030 208 268 1
shambhu@web.de
www.reiseantiquitaeten.de
Mon-Fri 12:00-19:00; Sat 11:00-15:00
U2 Sophie-Charlotte-Platz

Travel enables collecting. If you think about it, we all bring something home from our journeys whether it is a postcard, a classy fridge magnet or chewing gum. Reiseanitquitäten collects and sells things that relate to travel like old luggage as well as globes and small souvenirs. In addition to this, you will find paintings from the 1940s and other art and design objects.

SCHÖNE ALTE GLÄSER

Suarezstraße 58
030 323 811 1
amanda@ schoene-alte-glaeser.de
www.schoene-alte-glaeser.de
Mon-Fri 11:00-18:00; Sat 11:00-15:00
U2 Sophie-Charlotte-Platz

Now this is what I call a focus! Brigitte
von Kuhlberg has been collecting glasses
for the past 30 years and she shares her
collection in her shop on Suarezstraße, the
long mile of antique shops in Berlin. From
liqueur glasses to old Biedermeier wine
glasses, Murano glass objects, this place
is a glass paradise where any size or style
can be found. And if not, just ask for it and
it will be sourced.

ZEITLOS

Kantstraße 17
030 315 156 31
info@ zeitlos-berlin.de
www.zeitlos-berlin.de
Mon-Sat 10:00-19:00
U1 Uhlandstraße

In the 90s when Uwe opened Zeitlos,
vintage and secondhand furniture was
not as stylish as it is today. Moreover, it
was difficult to find original pieces, there
were just a few art galleries around so
he decided to focus on Bauhaus and is
keeping that tradition today. All the pieces
at Zeitlos are collector's items: Thonet,
Mies van der Rohe and other big names
are represented in this showroom with
iconic pieces and original fabrics. Even
the interior resembles the 30s, the floor
is covered with linoleum and there are
bakelite lamps. Timeless design indeed,
and one of the most important shops in
Berlin for vintage furniture. Not to
be missed!

ACCESSORIES & AMBIENTE

Bürknerstraße 39
030 634 132 12
Mon-Fri 13:00-20:00; Sat 12:00-17:00
U8 Schönleinstraße

Owned by a Polish ex-journalist for South American affairs, this place is actually more of a space for social encounters where you can come after work and sit in front of the fireplace than simply a shop. Equipped with a regular-sized bar, you'll be served coffee or tea.

With a passion for old things, the owner started collecting paintings, vases, ceramics and other antique objects from flea markets until he decided to open up this place and share his hobby with the public. The cabinets are a highlight, together with the Art Deco lamps, wall clocks, Victorian and Gründerzeit furniture located in the back of the shop.

ADLER

Weichselstraße 15
030 832 172 24
Mon-Sat 12:00-20:00
U7 Rathaus Neukölln

This street where Adler is located in Neukölln can be nicknamed as "the secondhand land". An all-electric-appliances store like Adler must be included on the list.

BERLIN-TRÖDEL

Pannierstraße 10A
030 780 805 43
Mon-Sat 10:00-19:00
U7&U8 Hermannplatz

This shop covers all secondhand categories including washing machines and fridges and offers cellar clearances together with transportation services.

DAKKOUR ELEKTRONIC

Erkstraße 21
030 260 301 41
Mon-Sat 10:00-18:30
U7 Rathaus Neukölln

Microwaves, bikes and huge restaurant-size fridges and freezers. Things are piled on top of each other, but this could be THE place to find that electronic appliance no other shop has.

EKSTASE 51
LICHT & DESIGN

Friedelstraße 51
030 850 756 11
ekstase51@googlemail.com
www.ekstase51.de
Tue-Fri 15:00-19:00; Sat 14:00-18:00
U7&U8 Hermannplatz

A labyrinth of vintage treasures, the shop was opened inside a flat and so you will find six rooms, each with its own theme like the Teak room with Danish furniture; the 70s room with lamps, vases and kitchen accessories; the 50s room predominantly with GDR furniture; and the showroom with designer brand furniture. This store intrigues you from the very beginning with its wide-ranging selection of incredible objects. The chic and the crazy, the elegant, and the brightly colored, it is simply surprising. When you add that Sabine Descher doesn't earn her living from this shop, it is just her hobby, you appreciate it even more.

HAUSHALTSGERÄTE-PETER WIENS

Sonnenallee 38
030 624 203 9
haushaltsgeraete-peter-wiens@gmx.net
Mon-Fri 10:00-18:00; Sat 10:00-14:00
U7 &U8 Hermannplatz

Refrigerators, washing machines, dishwashers and plenty of stoves! Secondhand gas cookers are considered rare because they are hard to clean after years of use, but Peter Wiens thoroughly scrubs them so they sparkle. You'll get a six-month warranty for any appliance you leave with.

TAMIM

Hobrechtstraße 6
030 624 331 7
info@gebrauchte-elektrogeraete-berlin.de
www.gebrauchte-elektrogeraete-berlin.de
Mon-Fri 9:00-18:00
U7&U8 Hermannplatz

Active since 1977, their motto is: we sell everything that has a plug. All the appliances come from private houses and are sold at three times less than the price of new ones. The talkative and nice woman who owns the shop brought me up to date on what is going on in the neighborhood so a visit to the store also serves as an introduction to the history and current happenings of the area. She concludes our talk by saying it is now hard to find "the good old secondhand items".

ONLY IN
BERLIN

Flea Markets
East-West Nostalgia

NOSTALGIA INITIALLY MEANT HOMESICKNESS AND WAS CONSIDERED TO BE A MEDICAL CONDITION, A CRAVING TO RETURN TO THE NATIVE LAND. NOSTALGIA TODAY HAS MORE TO DO WITH DAY-DREAMING ABOUT THE PAST, TIME SITTING STILL AND MEMORIES TRIGGERED BY THE SMELL OF A PERFUME OR THE TICK OF A CLOCK.

But how did its meaning change? Although I believe there are some feelings that you can't explain, the most plausible explanation I have heard relates to the pace of technological innovation. This makes sense because our bodies and souls are essentially slow to adapt to change and to the speed of technological developments, nostalgia becomes our way back into the comfortable and familiar.

The fact that Berlin was separated for so long into East and West has accelerated the feeling of nostalgia among its inhabitants, the urge to know and even experience life on the other side of the 'wall'. This doesn't apply only to Easterners craving a better life in the West, but also to Westerners curious about life in the East and admiring the designs and products originating there. This phenomenon bears the name 'ostalgia' and this is why in Berlin you will find many stores to buy clothing, objects, packaging (like tomato sauce jars, etc.) and furniture from the GDR.

There is a large group who work on keeping these objects visible as a reminder of those times. And if you really want to see what a GDR flat used to look like, type Museumswohnung WBS 70 into your Google search bar and make an appointment to see it for free!

A second important area of nostalgia in Berlin, is the 'Golden 20s', the time of sophisticated culture when the legendary Wintergarten Hall was blooming with its variety shows, burlesque and swing parties. It was simply a glamorous time in spite of the difficult economic situation and people today still long for it – see swing revival and the Burlesque Sauvage parties. Still in the day, the altbau apartments that were built in those times are in high demand and their style and ambiance stimulate people to search for the old even more intensely.

While what triggers nostalgic feelings is unique for every person because of his or her own unique past, I couldn't help but notice that there are similarities in lifestyle, musical taste, likes and dislikes among people who seek nostalgia.

Let see some of nostalgia's embodiments in Berlin...

KREUZBERG

ARENA HALLEN-TRÖDELMARKT

Eichenstraße 4
030 533 20 30
www.arena-berlin.de
Sat-Sun 10:00-18:00
U1 Schlesisches Tor

Arena is the electronic app wonderland (app as in appliances not as in smartphones). You can find everything you need from the most common requests; kitchen appliances and sinks, lamps, ovens, vacuum cleaners, rugs and paintings, and bicycles to the most unusual ones; disco balls, old phones, wheelchairs, old cash registers, gas pumps and accordions. The place entices you with its oddities.

MOTZ-DER LADEN

Friedrichstraße 226
030 691 343 2
motz@motz-berlin.de / www.motz-berlin.de
Mon-Fri 11:00-19:00; Sat 11:00-17:00
U6 Kochstraße

Motz is a charity for the homeless. Among other activities and acts of kindness, Motz publishes a newspaper entirely created by the people it helps. Buying from this store, as you've probably already guessed, means helping the homeless get back on track and re-enter society. Anything from coffee cups to sofas arrive in the store through donations and the prices are not decided by the organization, but on the principle of: Who has little, pays little, who has more, pays more.

MARHEINEKE MARKTHALLE

Marheinekeplatz
030 398 961
www.meine-markthalle.de
Sat-Sun 10:00-16:00 (Sun only from April)
U7 Gneisenaustrasse

Attached to a gourmet indoor market that is also not to be missed, the Marheineke flea market has a bunch of stalls owned by neighborhood locals and offers second hand stuff in a cosy atmosphere.

NOWKÖLLN-FLOWMARKT

Maybachufer
www.nowkoelln.de
every 3rd Sunday of the month
U8 Schönleinstraße

This little market is made up of private secondhand sellers, art and hand-made items, live music but no vintage. The neighbors have fought to close this Sunday market, so let's see how long it survives. This is the same street where the wonderful Turkish market takes place on Tuesdays and Fridays where Turkish delis are combined with live bands, thousands of textiles, fresh vegetables and fruits. Something not to be missed!

PETER´S WERKSTATT

Skalitzer Straße 46b
030 618 654 9
info@peterswerkstatt.de
peterswerkstatt.de
Mon-Fri 9:00 – 18:00
U1 Görlitzer Bahnhof

The charming interwar radios and TVs displayed here are unfortunately not for sale, but if you feel nostalgic you can rent them or simply drop by to admire their looks. These attractive, authentic machines are frequently used as props in Hollywood movies, book fairs, fashion shows, museums and galleries. The evolution of technology has forced this shop to change its mission from a common radio store to a rent and repair workshop.

RADIO ART

Zossener Straße 2
030 693 943 5
info@radio-art.de / www.radio-art.de
Tue & Fri: 12:00-18:00, Sat 10:00-13:00
U7 Gneisenaustraße

Telefunken, the German radio and television apparatus company, founded in Berlin in 1903, enabled Hitler's voice to reach the population. Roberts was the most successful portable radio in the 30s. And you can still touch, use and buy these devices. Radio Art collects many of the famous radio models and sells them to people who remember the old times. Why are these radios still so appreciated? Answer: "Why do people like and buy vintage cars? It is an art".

AMITOLA

Krossener Straße 35
030 862 049 84
inespavlou@yahoo.de
www. amitola-berlin.de
Mon-Sat 10:00-18:30
U5 Samariterstraße

Amitola is a combination of playground, family café and secondhand shop. The idea grew from a tiny secondhand shop that sometimes offered a cup of coffee or a space for mothers to get together, hold courses or workshops and have children's book readings. The blend of old and new kids' brands, handmade items, wooden toys, and children's books, provides everything you might wish for in the same place--both pricey and cheap. You can always try to negotiate the price if you are buying many items. A place for neighborhood regulars.

ANTIK UND TRÖDELMARKT AM OSTBAHNHOF

**Erich-Steinfurth-Straße
(between Ostbahnhof and Kaufhof)
030 290 020 10
www.oldthing.de
Sun 9:00-17:00
S Ostbahnhof**

This market has the most nostalgic feeling and influence of all because it is really equipped with 'the old'. Focusing on German history, the market at Ostbahnhof offers old *Der Spiegel* or *Die Woche* publications, postcards and photographs, stamps and envelopes from 1933 on, pins and medals from the World War I and mini collectible ceramics. You'll experience the old artifacts and touch a bit of history here.

BOXHAGENER PLATZ FLEA MARKET

**Boxhagener Platz
www.boxhagenerplatz.de
Sat 8:00-13:30; Sun 10:00-18:00
S+U1 Warschauer Straße**

If it's Saturday, you'll find a farmer's market: flowers, fresh fruits and good cheese. On Sunday, you'll find a classic flea market: heaps of lamps, vinyls, cupboards and junk.

The park in the middle offers quite a show; circus tricks, people lying in the sun, others having a picnic. Self-proclaimed artists will enchant your ears with song. You should definitely stop at Café Pavilion, on one of the corners of the 'platz', buy yourself a lemonade and enjoy the show.

RAW FLEA MARKET

Revaler Straße 99
0176 687 922 21
www.raw-flohmarkt.de
Sun 10:00-18:00
S+U1 Warschauer Straße

RAW stands for a long German word: Reichsbahnausbesserungswerk. Meaning, that back in the old days, the space was a workshop for the national railroad where locomotives and wagons were repaired. Now it is a spot for special projects, nightclubs and one of Europe's biggest indoor skate parks.

Coincidently or not, 'RAW' fits the description of this relatively young flea market where private sellers have stalls near to heavily graffiti-covered walls and unfinished buildings and sell their aged belongings for low prices. A true Berlin scene rebelling against the age of cheap mass production.

ⓔⓔⓔ-ⓔⓔⓔ

ARKONAPLATZ FLEA MARKET

Arkonaplatz
030 786 976 4
www.troedelmarkt-arkonaplatz.de
Sun 10:00-16:00
U8 Bernauer Straße

The assortment at this little market is remarkable. For every home that needs a splash of vintage soul, this is one of the sweetest places to find it. What exactly are you offered? The usual flea market stuff, but the quality is generally better. The prices are slightly higher than at other markets, but then you need to pay a little more for the unique and the lovely.

ⓔⓔⓔ-ⓔⓔⓔ

MAUERPARK FLEA MARKET

Bernauer Straße 63-64
0176 29 25 00 21
info@mauerpark.de
www.mauerparkmarkt.de
Sun 8:00-18:00
U8 Bernauer Straße

The Mauerpark Flea Market is THE flea market in Berlin. Locals, tourists and visitors make sure to set aside time to visit this market each Sunday. A place of history, the massive market stands where many people were killed during the time of the wall. Some reminders of the terror are still there so if you walk a couple of meters up the street you will see the Berlin Wall Memorial and that may give you goose bumps.

Besides the hundreds of stands, the crowd spontaneously gathers at 15:00 for a karaoke session that represents the highlight of the day.

The market is a bit too renowned, so prices are high and lots of new handmade items and various forms of art have crept in among the real vintage items. I suggest you either arrive early at 8:00 for the good stuff or at dusk for the leftovers at low prices. Oh, and you can be sure to enjoy delicious food.

PHILATELIE

Kollwitzstraße 93
030 442 633 3
philatelie.heinemann@web.de
Mon-Thu 9:00-13:00 and 14:00-17:30;
Fri 9:00-13:00, afternoons by appointment
U2 Eberswalder Straße

Previously a shelter for cats and dogs, Philatelie now houses some of the most valuable stamps and envelopes. One of the first ever issued stamps (from 6th of May 1840 in London), called the 'penny black', is concealed there but by paying around €1000 you could own it. "Long time ago, stamps were considered to be a window into the world--seeing one of them coming from a far off country made one dream of distant shores, but now TV has replaced this pleasure and we have more powerful windows into the world. But still, a stamp can tell a lot about history", says Mr. Heinemann, the owner of the shop.

REMBETIS

Oderberger Straße 35
030 648 351 41
rembetis@live.de/ www.rembetis1.de
Mon-Sat 14:00-19:00
U2 Eberswalder Straße

Georgios Velissarios and his wife used to live in a three-room apartment, one of which was completely filled with bikes--80 bikes! One day they found they couldn't possibly move around the house anymore, so they opened Rembetis.

Rembetis possesses some real beauties! Old-style bikes coming mostly from Italy, France and Germany: Adler, Miller, Singer, Dayton Ohio, Diamant, Mifa, Excelsius. The collection is like a museum of more than 200 bikes. The oldest dates from 1886, a Liberator, and the racing bikes date from 1980. Some of the bikes were found abandoned immediately after the wall fell.

Mr. Velissarios, originally from Crete, has been collecting vintage bicycles for 50 years and loves them as if they were his babies. That's why money is not enough. Before you can buy one of his bikes, Georgios first has to make sure that you are a true bike lover yourself, capable of taking care of the object of desire. The shop can also restore and renew classics.

They want Rembetis to become a meeting point for bike lovers so they are thinking about opening a café soon.

VEB ORANGE

Oderberger Straße 29
030 978 868 86
info@veborange.de
www.veb-orange.de/ veborange.de
Mon-Sat 10:00-20:00
U2 Eberswalder Straße

This one is nicknamed 'the museum-shop'. VEB orange is a GDR paradise with everything from little collectible toys, games, and lamps to kitchenware and clothing. A very funny store with a strongly nostalgic atmosphere. The owner started collecting when he was a kid and as he couldn't possibly part with these things, he kept everything...no wonder his store looks like an over-caffeinated East-meets-West now. It's almost a collection of memories because he likes to tell the story of every object in the room. Fun fact: he borrows the nostalgic glasses, marmalade cups and ketchup containers for film and photo shootings. This is a place where you have to search in order to find what you want, but this makes the hunt enjoyable.

'I hope to carry on with my hobby, keep finding valuable collections and be in contact with people sharing the same thoughts.
I have a great job!'

REINHARD HEINEMANN, PHILATELIE

Philatelie

Reinhard Heinemann, a proud collector of impressive stamps and envelopes, was born in Berlin and opened Philatelie 20 years ago, right after the wall was torn down. I like to say he is collecting pieces of history. Back then and even now, in a nostalgic way, stamps were considered to be windows into the world as there was no other media access to knowing things.

Heinemann's grandfather was a stamp collector himself and that's where his passion came from. Very soon, this led him to join a stamp collectors club for kids when he was young. His eyes became bigger and bigger at the sight of a stamp coming from far-far away, giving him the feeling of holding the whole world in his hands. Later on, he worked for an art agency and then decided to change jobs. As he was already a stamp collector, he thought of marrying his passion with business.

"Stamps used to be a propaganda medium, glorifying Hitler, and now by looking at their fine drawings and writing, one can understand more", says Heinemann. He owns many of these propagandist stamps but moreover, the envelopes are the ones who carry the highest value: "Hitler used to send back the envelopes celebrating things he was against or in the best case, he used to cover the icon with black ink".

Heinemann buys the stamps and envelopes mostly from special auctions, but often the collectors - who are either in need of money or elderly and wish to make sure somebody will value their beloved items - come here to sell their collections.

"I hope to carry on with my hobby, keep finding valuable collections and be in contact with people sharing the same thoughts. I have a great job!" concludes Heinemann

ANTIKE BAUELEMENTE

Lehrter Straße 25-26
030 394 309 3
mail@antike-bauelemente-berlin.de
www.antike-bauelemente-berlin.de
Wed & Sat 10:00-14:00
S Hauptbahnhof

Is it beautiful? I haven't decided yet if this word is the best description, but it is in the deepest sense a place of hidden treasures, a place of fascination. Filled with over 2000 doors, windows, and decorative elements taken from what used to be Art Nouveau or Grunderzeit buildings, stairs, tiles, planks, brass, iron stoves, fireplaces, they all sit in a backyard with plants growing around them. These items were parts of buildings that have been demolished for economic reasons, and have been being rescued by Wolfram Liebchen for more than 25 years.

One can even find out the background history of the doors that are drunkenly pitched into the barn. It's usually written on an attached label or hidden in the back office of Mr. Liebchen.

ANTIK UND BUCHMARKT AM BODEMUESUM

Am Kupfergraben 1 on the Museum Island
0171 710 166 2
www. antik-buchmarkt.de
Sat 10:00-17:00, Sun 10:00-16:00
S Oranienburger Straße

A classy flea market located in one of the most noble areas of Berlin –where the channel bends to embrace the Bode Museum. Here, the highlights are the paintings, jewels, curios, porcelain and some DDR reminders (as always): gas masks (?!), CCCP belts, hats, pins and military decorations. For the more refined souls, look for a jewellery stand run by an older couple--they sell irresistible Italian mosaic brooches from the 1960s. The market is a pleasant stroll before going to a fairytale-for-adults play at the Märchenhütte Theater on the other side of the river.

ANTIKFLAIR CAFÉ & MÖBEL

Grunewaldstraße 10
030 666 206 20
info@antikflair.de / www.antikflair.de
Mon-Fri 11:00-19:00; Sat 11:00-16:00
U7 Kleistpark

So here's the plan: you take a seat, drink a cup of coffee in the sunshine (hard to achieve in Berlin) and if you fall in love with the surroundings, they write the bill both for the coffee and the antique Biedermeier furniture you liked. Deal?

CAFÉ BILDERBUCH

Akazienstraße 28
030 787 060 57
info@cafe-bilderbuch.de
www.cafe-bilderbuch.de
Mon-Sat 9:00-24:00; Sun 10:00-24:00
U7 Eisenacher Straße

I mentioned earlier that Berliners are all about extensive breakfasts. One of the loveliest places to accomplish your Sunday duty as a genuine citizen of the city is Café BilderBuch that literally translates as Café Picture Book. An art gallery, café and library in the same time, you can exchange the book you have finished reading with a new one from the shelves. Nobody supervises you, but there is one condition: you must pick a book that is the same size as the one you leave there. Otherwise the shelves will start looking empty...

CLASSIC REMISE. MEILENWERK

Wiebestraße 36-37
030 364 078 0
berlin@remise.de/ www.remise.de
Mon-Sat 8:00-20:00; Sun 10:00-20:00
U7 Mierendorffplatz

For all of you who have petrol running through your veins, there is Meilenwerk. If you are crazy about retro cars, or just dreamy about a dolce vita lifestyle, Meilenwerk offers 16,000 square metres of all that under one roof. You'll find iconic models from the 60s: Jaguar, Porsche, Mercedes Benz, Aston Martin in cabriolet versions or not, no matter the name, they are all elegant and very rare!

This is not only a repair shop or a place for retro car-related gear, but also a meeting point for those passionate about style.

TIERGARTEN

Straße des 17. Juni
030 265 500 96
info@berliner-troedelmarkt.de
www.berliner-troedelmarkt.de
Sat-Sun 10:00-17:00
S Tiergarten

Tiergarten, the first-ever Berlin flea market, opened in 1973 and looks like a romantic kind of bazaar. Door handles from Berlin's 1880 castles, gramophones, old typing machines, Art Nouveau and naturalist paintings stand side-by-side with a variety of thrift objects from teddy bears to computer games, arts and crafts.

UHREN & KUNST BISCHOFF

Pestalozzistraße 54
030 323 216 3
uhren.bischoff@berlin.de
www.uhren-bischoff.de
Mon-Fri 13:00-18:00; Sat 10:00-13:00
U2 Sophie-Charlotte-Platz

When I think of old clocks I always remember my grandfather's table clock that had the world map engraved on the back of its rounded golden case. I can still picture it on the dining room table. Uhren & Kunst reminds me of that, but the shop is really state of the art where clocks are concerned whether it's Vienna wall clocks, French and English table clocks, grandfather clocks or wristwatches. The clocks all come from a distant past--1840-1920--and are treated with love and care by Mr. Bischoff who, for the last 30 years, has collected and repaired them. An exclusive vintage watches sales and repair shop.

ANTIK & TRÖDELMARKT RICHARDSTRASSE

Richardstraße 105
030 818 948 35
Mon-Fri 10:00-18:00
U7 Neukölln

There is no point in trying to sugar coat it. This open air market on Richardstraße looks like a garbage dump because the objects lie scattered around. Lamps, detergent?!, luggage and trophies of forgotten events and people. I did find one little treasure there: an old wooden box of French chocolate liqueur. No, but seriously, you might not be disappointed after digging in. But be prepared to rummage.

DIE TELLER GOTTES

Bruno-Bauer-Str. 22
030 263 029 87
die-teller-gottes@arcor.de
Mon-Fri 11:00-18:00
U7 Neukölln

Literally translated as a social/charity department store, the place is huge and fusty. Unsorted and packed with everything from teaspoons to kitchen cupboards, sofas and books, it looks like it is about to burst onto the street. Handbags are hanging where bottles would usually stand in the bar, but it is a nice view for anyone who stops there for a cup of coffee and a rest from shopping.

SING BLACKBIRD

Sanderstraße 11
030 548 450 51
singblackbirdvintage@gmail.com
www.singblackbird.com
Mon-Sun 10:30-20:00
U8 Schönleinstraße

Recently opened in the Berlin vintage scene, this café plus clothing store is a breath of fresh air. Owned by a Croatian, Diana Durdic and Tasha Arana, a Californian, Sing Blackbird originated at a birthday party where the two women brought vintage clothes and home-baked cakes while the crowd went crazy. The thinking behind their shop: vintage shops are overpriced and trödel-stores are too trashy, so Sing Blackbird is in between. Looking cute and well designed, it is indeed making beautiful and up-cycled vintage items affordable.

Moreover, everything that comes from the kitchen is home-made: cheesecake with pumpkin pie topping, organic scones and vegan breakfasts, American pancakes. Wednesday is classical movie night and if you are lucky you might also find an exhibition on. Vintage store, café, gallery and party place all in one. What more can one wish for?

BERLIN
MAPS

The following collection of maps will help you navigate your way around Berlin's secondhand and vintage shops and markets. Each corresponds to the zones used in the preceding chapters – Kreuzberg, Friedrichshain, Prenzlauer Berg, Mitte, Schöneberg, Charlottenburg and Neukölln.

Each entry is listed under its category and the colour of the icon on the map corresponds to that category, with sites marked by diamonds:

CLOTHES AND ACCESSORIES

BOOKS, MUSIC & MEMORABILIA

HOME & INTERIORS

ONLY IN BERLIN

Each map has a QR code. If you have a smart phone, you can simply scan the code to link to online versions of the maps on Google which will help you find your way around. These are regularly updated to keep pace with Berlin's evolving secondhand and vintage landscape.

CLOTHING

1 CHECKPOINT & CINEMA
Mehringdamm 41
Mon-Wed 11:00-19:00; Thu-Fri
11:00-20:00; Sat 11:00-19:00

2 COLOURS
Bergmannstraße 102
Mon-Fri 11:00 – 19:00;
Sat 12:00 – 19:00

3 JUMBO SECOND HAND
Wiener Straße 63
Mon-Sat 11:00-19:30

4 KINDERSACHEN AUS 2. HAND
Graefestraße 1
Mon-Fri 11:00-18:00

5 LINDT
Körtestraße 16
Mon-Fri 12:00-18:00; Sat freestyle

6 ROSENROT
Eisenbahnstraße 48
Mon-Fri 10:30-18:30; Sat 10:30-14:30

7 SECOND-HAND PARADISE
Adalbertstraße 17
Mon-Sat 12:00-20:00

8 ST-STORE BERLIN
Karl-Kunger-Straße 54
Tue-Fri 12:00-19:00; Sat 12:00-18:00

9 STYLO
Hagelbergerstraße 52
Mon-Fri 11:00-18:00; Sat 12:00-16:00

BOOKS & MUSIC

10 ANTIQUARIAT KALLIGRAMM
Oranienstraße 28
Mon-Fri 12:00-18:00,
Sat: 12:00-16:00

11 ART ET ANTIQUITES
Zossener Straße 48
Mon-Fri 16:00-19:00

12 BIKE:CO:HOLICS
Gneisenaustraße 67
Mon-Fri 11:00-19:00

13 EXTRA-BUCH MODERNES ANTIQUARIAT
Mehringdamm 66
Mon-Fri 10:00-20:00;
Sat 10:00-18:00

14 FAIR EXCHANGE
Dieffenbachstraße 58
Mon-Fri 11:00-19:00; Sat 10:00-18:00

15 HAMMET
Friesenstraße 27
Mon-Fri 10:00-20:00; Sat 9:00-18:00

16 KUBI'S BIKE SHOP
Falckensteinstraße 35
Mon-Fri 10:00-19:00,
Sat 10:00-16:00

17 KULTGUT
Wrangelstraße 45
Mon-Fri 13:00-19:00; Sat 11:00-16:00

18 LONG PLAYER-VINYL LIVING ROOM
Graefestraße 80
Tue, Thu-Sat 12:00-20:00;
Wed 12:00-24:00

19 MODERN GRAPHICS
Oranienstraße 22
Mon-Fri 11:00-20:00; Sat 10:00-19:30

20 MÜBIGGANG
Oranienstraße 14a
Tue-Sat 14:00-19:00

21 OTHERLAND
Bergmannstraße 25
Mon-Fri 11:00-19:00; Sat 11:00-17:00

22 PIATTO FORTE
Schlesische Straße 38a
Mon-Fri 12:00-20:00; Sat 12:00-17:00

23 SATORI-RECORDS
Wrangelstraße 64
Mon-Fri 14:00-19:00; Sat 12:00-16:00

24 TAUSENDUNDEINBUCH
Gneisenaustraße 60
Mon-Fri 11:00-19:00; Sat 11:00-14:00

25 UMBRAS KURIOSITÄTEN-KABINETT
Graefestraße 18
Mon-Fri 14:00-17:00

HOME & INTERIORS

26 ADLER ANTIK
Urbanstraße 124
Mon-Fri 10:00-19:00; Sat 10:00-17:00

27 GUERILLIAZ
Gneisenaustraße 55
Mon-Fri 11:00-19:00; Sat 11:00-16:00

28 KLASSIKERFUNDUS
Südstern 6
Tu-Fr 12-19, Sat: 12-16

29 KOMFORT 36
Schlesische Straße 38a
Thu-Fri 14:00-19:30; Sat 13:00-18:00

30 KRAMARI
Gneisnaustraße 91
Tue-Fri 14:00-19:00; Sat 12:00-17:00

31 NESTHOCKER
Graefestraße 75
Tue-Fri 14:00-19:00; Sat 12:00-15:00

32 POLSTEREI&GALERIE
Graefestraße 90
Mon-Fri 10:00-18:00; Sat 11:00-16:00

33 PONY HÜTCHEN
Pücklerstraße 33
Mon-Sat 15:00-20:00

34 SCHUBLADEN
Körtestraße 26
Tue-Fri 11:00-19:00; Sat 11:00-16:00

35 SHÖWRAUM
Schönleinstraße 3
open from morning to late evening
– appointment advisable

ONLY IN BERLIN

36 ARENA HALLENTRÖDELMARKT
Eichenstraße 4
Sat-Sun 10:00-18:00

37 MARHEINEKE MARKTHALLE
Marheinkeplatz
Sat-Sun 10:00-16:00

38 MOTZ-DER LADEN
Friedrichstraße 226
Mon-Fri 11:00-19:00; Sat 11:00-17:00

39 NOWKÖLLN-FLOWMARKT
Maybachufer
Every 3rd Sunday of the month

40 PETER'S WERKSTATT
Skalitzer Straße 46b
Mon-Fri 9:00 – 18:00

41 RADIO ART
Zossener Straße 2
Tue & Fri: 12:00-18:00,
Sat 10:00-13:00

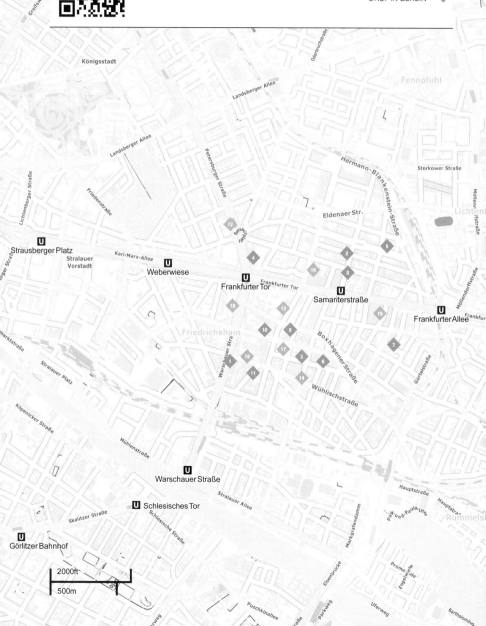

FRIEDRICHSHAIN

CLOTHES ◆
BOOKS & MUSIC ◆
HOME & INTERIORS ◆
ONLY IN BERLIN ◆

CLOTHES

(1) A&V MICHAELIS
Warschauer Straße 62
Mon-Fri 11:00-19:00; Sat 11:00-16:00

(2) BERLINER MODEINSTITUT
Samariterstraße 31
Mon-Sat 12:00-19:00

(3) GEILE JACKEN
Krossener Straße 24
Tue-Fri 15:00-19:00; Sat 13:00-18:00

(4) HUMANA
Frankfurter Tor 3
Mon-Fri 10:00-20:00

(5) JIBOO
Bänschstraße 77
Mon-Fri 10:00-18:00; Sat 10:00-16:00

(6) KLEIDER-MOTTE
Krossener Straße 29
Mon-Fri 11:00-19:00; Sat 12:00-16:00

(7) OSCAR
Müggelstraße 11a
Mon-Thu 9:30-18:00; Fri 9:30-15:00

(8) PARIS SECOND HAND
Samariterstraße 6
Mon-Fri 10:00-19:00; Sat 10:00-14:00

(9) ROCKING CHAIR
Gabriel-Max-Straße 13
Mon-Fri 12:00-19:00; Sat 10:00-16:00

(10) SIR HENRY&MY FEET
Grünberger Straße 37&47
Mon-Sat 10:00-20:00

(11) TRASH-SCHICK
Wühlischstraße 31
Mon-Sat 12:00-20:00

BOOKS & MUSIC

(12) A&V SECOND-BIKE
Petersburger Straße 74
Mon-Fri 10:00-19:00;
Sat 10:00-16:00

(13) ANTIQUARIAT IN FRIEDRICHSHAIN
Niederbarnimstraße 13
Tue-Fri 14:00-18:00; Sat 12:00-18:00

(14) ANTIQUARIAT MATTHIAS WAGNER
Wühlischstraße 22|23
Mon-Fri 15:00-19:00

(15) ANTIQUARIAT WEIGELT
Proskauerstraße 4
Wed-Fri 16:00-20:00;
Sat 14:00-18:00

(16) AUDIO-IN
Libauer Straße 19
Mon-Fri 14:00-20:00;
Sat 12:00-18:00

(17) O-TON RECORDSTORE
Krossener Straße 18
Mon-Sat 13:00-20:00

(18) SECOND-BIKE UND SOUND CAFÉ AN & VERKAUF
Warschauer Straße 12
Mon-Sat 10:00-22:00

(19) SPARBUCH
Finowstraße 5
Wed-Fri 19:00-20:00

Prenzlauer Berg

Greifswalder Straße

Greifswalder Straße

Knipfrodestraße

Grenzstraße

Storkower Straße

Weißenseer Weg

Hohenschönhauser Straße

Oderbruchstraße

Königsstadt

Fennpfuhl

Landsberger Allee

Landsberger Allee

Storkower Straße

Lichtenberg

Hermann-Blankenstein-Straße

Friedenstraße

Peterburger Straße

Eldenaer Str.

Möllendorfstraße

Lichtenberger Straße

Beskidenstraße

U Strausberger Platz

Stralauer
Vorstadt

Karl-Marx-Allee **23**

U Weberwiese

22

U Frankfurter Tor

Frankfurter Tor

U Samariterstraße

25

24

Möllendorfstraße

U Frankfurter Allee

Frankfur

marktstraße

Friedrichshain

Warschauer Stra

21

28

Boxhagener Straße

27

Stralauer Platz

Wühlischstraße

26

Gürtelstraße

Köpenicker Straße

29

Mühlenstraße

U Warschauer Straße

Stralauer Allee

Hauptstraße

Hauptstraße

U Schlesisches Tor

Skalitzer Straße

Schlesische Straße

Markgrafendamm

Park-und-Paula-Ufer

Rummels

U Görlitzer Bahnhof

2000ft

500m

Eisenbrücke

Parkweg

Promenade
Engeldamm

Uferweg

Bartholomäusstraße

Maxweg

Puschkinallee

Alt-Treptow

HOME & INTERIORS

20 A&V WASCHBÄR
Kopernikusstraße 12
Mon-Fri 10:00–19:00;
Sat 10:00-16:00

21 GRÜNBERGER AN&VERKAUF
Grünberger Straße 44
Mon-Fri 10:00-19:00; Sat 10:00-17:00

22 KUNST UND ANTIQUITÄTEN
Schreinerstraße 64a

23 ORIGINAL IN BERLIN
Karl-Marx-Allee 94
Mon-Fri 11:00-19:00; Sat 12:00-16:00

24 PIRA X - BERLIN
Niederbarnimstraße 20
Mon, Tue, Fri, Sat 14:00-20:00

25 TECHNISCHER AN&VERKAUF
Frankfurter Allee 68
Mon-Fri 10-18; Sat 10:00-14:00

ONLY BERLIN

26 AMITOLA
Krossener Straße 35
Mon-Sat 10:00-18:30

27 ANTIK UND TRÖDELMARKT AM OSTBAHNHOF
Erich-Steinfurth-Straße (between
Ostbahnhof and Kaufhof)
Sun 9:00-17:00

28 BOXHAGENER PLATZ FLEA MARKET
Boxhagener Platz
Sat 8:00-13:30; Sun 10:00-18:00

29 RAW FLEA MARKET
Revaler Straße 99
Sun 10:00-18:00

PRENZLAUER BERG

CLOTHES ◆
BOOKS & MUSIC ◆
HOME & INTERIORS ◆
ONLY IN BERLIN ◆

CLOTHING

1 BLUE EYES
Eberswalder Straße 23
Mon-Fri 11:00-18:00; Sat 10:00-16:00

2 COU-COU
Winsstraße 31
Tue-Sat 12:00-18:30

3 HILLY'S BERLIN
Kollwitzstraße 39
Mon-Sat starting at 11:00

4 LUNETTES BRILLENAGENTUR
Marienburger Straße 11
Mon-Fri 12:00-20:00;
Sat 12:00-18:00

5 MEINS&DEINS THE REAL FLASHBACK
Danzigerstraße 38
Mon-Sat 11:00-20:00

6 NYX
Zionskirchstraße 40
Tue-Fri 13:00-20:00; Sat 12:00-17:00

7 OPTIKING
Eberswalder Straße 34
Mon-Sat 12:00-20:00

8 PAUL'S BOUTIQUE
Oderbergerstraße 45&47
Mon-Sat 12:00-20:00

9 SCHNEEWITTE
Hufelandstraße 12
Mon-Fri 11:00-18:30; Sat 11:00-14:00

10 SECONDHAND
Kastanienallee 6
Mon-Fri 11:00-20:00; Sat 11:00-16:00

11 SENTIMENTAL JOURNEY
Husemannstraße 2
Mon-Sat 12:00-19:00

12 SOEUR
Marienburger Straße 24
Mon-Fri 11:00-19:00; Sat 11:00-18:00

13 STEIFEL KOMBINAT
Eberswalder Straße 21&22
Mon-Sat 10:00-22:00

14 THRIFT STORE
Kastanienallee 67
Mon-Sat 13:00-19:00

BOOKS & MISIC

15 BIBLIOTHECA CULINARIA
Zehdenicker Straße 16
Tu-Fri 11:00-19:00; Sat 11:00-16:00

16 BÖTZOW RAD BERLIN
Pasteurstraße 31
Mon-Fri 10:00-19:00;
Sat 10:00-16:00

17 FREAK OUT RECORDS
Prenzlauer Allee 49
Mon-Fri 11:00-19:30; Sat 11:00-16:00

18 MELTING POINT
Kastanienallee 55
Mon-Sat 12:00-20:00

19 MOGWA
Prenzlauer Allee 224
Mon-Fri 10:00-19:00;
Sat 10:00-16:00

20 MUSIKINSTRUMENTE & DESIGN
Schönhauser Allee 28
Mon-Fri 13:30-18:30; closed Thu

21 RE-CYCLE
Husemannstraße 33
Mon-Fri 11:00-20:00; Sat 11:00-18:00

22 SAINT GEORGE'S
Wörtherstraße 27
Mo-Fr: 11-20, Sat: 11-19

23 ST. PRENZL'BERG
Schönhauser Allee 41
Mon-Fri 10:30-20:00

SCHÖNHAUSER MUSIC I
Schönhauser Allee 70
Mon-Sat 11:00-20:00

SHAKESPEARE AND SONS
Raumerstraße 36
Mon-Sat 11:00-19:00

**SOZIALER BÜCHERLADEN IN BERLIN -
PRENZLAUER BERG**
Winsstraße 30
Mon-Fri 10:00-17:00;
Tue 10:00-19:00

HOME & INTERIORS

 A&V TECH
Eberswalder Straße 29
Mon-Fri: 11 - 19 Sa: 12-20

DER MÖBELLADEN
Wörther Straße 15
Tue-Fri 12:00-19:00; Sat 11:00-16:00

E-HAUS
Schliemannstraße 1
Mon-Sat 10:00-20:00

FRIEDRICHS LUST. KURIOSITÄTEN
Schönhauser Allee 8
Th&Fr: 15-19, Sat: 12-18

KOLLWITZ KABINET
Wörtherstraße 31
Mon-Fri 13:00–19:00; Sat 11:00-17:00

KUNST-A-BUNT
Wörther Straße 39
Mon-Fri 11:00-19:00; Sat 11:00-17:00

LAMPENMANUFAKTUR BERLIN
Rykestraße 51
Mon-Fri 12:00–19:00;
Sat 10:00-18:00

 MAGASIN
Lychener Straße 3
Mon-Fri 14:00-20:00;
Sat 12:00-18:00

 MÖBEL KOMBINAT BERLIN
Wolliner Straße 18-19
Mon-Sat 12:00-20:00

**OBJETS TROUVÉS NONCHALANTES
WOHNEN**
Rykestraße 32A
Wed-Sat 12:00–19:00

STUDIO ZIBEN
Danziger Straße 22
Tue-Sat 12:00-19:00

ZWISCHENZEIT
Raumerstraße 35
Mon-Fri 14:00-19:00

ONLY IN BERLIN

ARKONAPLATZ FLEA MARKET
Arkonaplatz
Sun 10:00-16:00

MAUERPARK FLEA MARKET
Bernauer Straße 63-64
Sun 8:00-18:00

PHILATELIE
Kollwitzstraße 93
Mon-Thu 9:00-13:00 and 14:00-
17:30; Fri 9:00-13:00, afternoons
by appointment

REMBETIS
Oderberger Straße 35
Mon-Sat 14:00-19:00

VEB ORANGE
Oderberger Straße 29
Mon-Sat 10:00-20:00

MITTE

CLOCKS ◆
BOOKS & MUSIC ◇
HOME & INTERIORS ◈
ONLY IN BERLIN ◆

Danzig

Bernauer
Mauerstreife

U Bernauer Straße

Schönhauser Allee

Oranienburger
Vorstadt

Bernauer Str.

Brunnenstraße

Weinbergsweg

U Senefelderplatz

Metz

Chausseestraße

Invalidenstraße

Gartenstraße

U Naturkundemuseum

◈ 16

◈ 17

◈ 18

U Rosenthaler Platz

◆ 9

◆ 7

Torstraße ◆ 2

Torstraße

Torstraße

Liniensstraße

◆ 13

U Rosa-Luxemburg-Platz

◆ 11

◆ 10

Auguststraße

Spandauer
Vorstadt

◆ 15

◆ 6

◆ 4

◆ 14

◆ 3

◆ 8

Scheunenviertel

U Weinmeisterstraße

◆ 1

◆ 5

U Oranienburger Tor

Oranienburger Str.

◆ 12

drich-
helm-
tadt

Reinhardtstraße

Friedrichstraße

Karl-Liebknecht-Straße

Alexanderstraße

U Alexanderplatz

Alt-Berlin

Grunerstraße

n

U Friedrichstraße

Spandauer Straße

Dorotheenstadt

Nikolaiviertel

U Klosterstraße

Unter den Linden

Unter den Linden

Molkmarkt

reeufer

U Brandenburger Tor

Behrenstraße

Französische Straße **U**

Friedrichswerder

Rolandufer

Jannowi

nstraße

1000ft

200m

Hausvogteiplatz **U**

Neukölln am
Wasser **U** Märkisches Museum

CLOTHING

**1 ANTIQUE VINTAGE JEWELRY.
OLIVER RHEINFRANK**
Linienstraße 44
Mon-Sat 11:00-19:00

2 ALEX VINTAGE STORE
Rosa-Luxemburg Straße 17
Mon-Fri 12:00-20:00;
Sat 12:00-20:00

3 BLITZ BOUTIQUE BERLIN
Krausnickstraße 23
Mon-Sat 12:00-20:00

4 CALYPSO
Rosenthalerstraße 23
Mon-Fri 12:00-20:00; Sat 12:00-18:00

5 CASH
Rosa-Luxemburg Straße 11
Mon-Fri 11:00-19:00; Sat 12:00-19:00

6 DAS NEUE SCHWARZ
Mulackstraße 37
Mon-Sat 12:00-20:00

7 GARMENTS
Linienstraße 204-205
Mon-Sat 12:00-19:00

8 GLANZSTÜCKE
Sophienstraße 7 – Hackesche Höfe
Mon-Sat 12:00-19:00

9 LUNETTES BRILLENAGENTUR
Torstraße 172
Mon-Fri 12:00-20:00; Sat 12:00-18:00

10 MADE IN BERLIN
Friedrichstraße 114 A
Mon-Fri 10:00-19:00;
Sat 12:00-20:00

11 O.F.T.
Chausseestraße 131B
Mon-Fri 13:00-20:00; Sat 13:00-18:00

12 RIANNA IN BERLIN
Große Hamburger Straße 25
Mon-Sat 12:00-19:00

13 SOMMERLADEN
Linienstraße 153
Mon-Fri 14:00-20:00; Sat 12:00-17:00

14 STERLING GOLD
Heckmann-Höfe, Oranienburger
Straße 32
Mon-Fri 12:00-20:00;
Sat 12:00-18:00

15 XVII OR DIX-SEPT
Steinstraße 17
Mon-Fri 11:00-19:00; Sat 11:00-17:00

BOOKS & MUSIC

16 THE RECORD STORE
Brunnenstraße 186
Mon-Sat 12:00-20:00

17 SOFORTBILD SHOP BERLIN
Brunnestraße 195
Mon-Fri 12:00-20:00;
Sat 12:00-18:00

18 UNTERWEGS
Torstraße 93
Tue-Fri 15:00-19:00; Sat 12:00-15:00

Voltastraße U

Eberswalder Straße U

Eberswalder Straße

Danzig

Brunnenstraße

**Rosenthaler
Vorstadt**

Bernauer Straße
Mauerstreifen

Bernauer Straße U

Schönhauser Allee

Bernauer Str.

**Oranienburger
Vorstadt**

Brunnenstraße

Weinbergsweg

Senefelderplatz U

Metze

hausseestr

25

2 Miles

Invalidenstraße

U
Naturkundemuseum

Gartenstraße

Rosenthaler Platz U

18

Torstr   ße

21

20

Torstraße

Torstraße

Linienstraße

Rosa-Luxemburg-Platz

Auguststraße

23

**Spandauer
Vorstadt**

Scheunenviertel

U
Weinmeisterstraße

drich-
nelm-
adt

U
Oranienburger Tor

Oranienburger Str.

22

Karl-Liebknecht-Straße

Alexanderstraße

Reinhardtstraße

Friedrichstraße

24

U
Alexanderplatz

Alt-Berlin

Grunerstraße

U
Friedrichstraße

Dorotheenstadt

Spandauer Straße

reuufer

Molk markt

Nikolaiviertel

U
Klosterstraße

Unter den Linden

Unter den Linden

Friedrichswerder

n

U
denburger Tor

Behrenstraße

Rolandufer

Jannowitz

nstraße

Französische Straße U

1000ft

200m

Friedrichstra

Hausvogteiplatz U

**Neukölln am
Wasser** U Märkisches Museum

CONTINUED

HOME & INTERIORS

19 **AUS ZWEITER HAND**
Torstraße 98
Mon-Fri 13:00-19:00

20 **FRIEDRICHS LUST SCHREIBER +
MOZEDLANI**
Schöenhauser Allee 8
Thu-Fri 15:00-19:00; Sat 12:00-18:00

21 **STUE**
Torstraße 70
Mon-Sat 12:00-19:00

22 **20TH CENTURY INTERIOR BERLIN**
Münzstraße 19 - 1st backyard
Tue-Sat 12:00-18:00 or by
appointment

23 **WAAHNSINN**
Rosenthaler Straße 17
Mon-Sat 9:00-18:00

ONLY BERLIN

24 **ANTIK UND BUCHMARKT AM
BODEMUESUM**
Am Kupfergraben 1 on the
Museum Island
Sat 10:00-17:00, Sun 10:00-16:00

25 **ANTIKE BAUELEMENTE**
Lehrter Straße 25-26
Wed and Sat 10:00-14:00

SCHÖNEBERG

CLOTHES ◆
BOOKS & MUSIC ◆
HOME & INTERIORS ◆
ONLY IN BERLIN ◆

CLOTHING

1 AUNES
Kolonnenstraße 3
Tue-Sat 14:00-18:00

2 FIRLEFANZ
Eisenacher Straße 75
Mon-Fri 14:30-18:30; Sat 11:00-15:00

3 LUMPEN PRINZESSIN
Kyffhäuserstraße 19
Mon-Fri 10:30-18:30; Sat 11:00-15:00

4 MIMI
Goltzstraße 5
Mon-Fri 12:00-19:00; Sat 11:00-16:00

5 SILHOUETTE IM FARBENREIGEN
Belziger Straße 19
Mon 14:00-19:00; Tue-Fri
12:00-19:00; Sat 11:00-16:00

6 TROLLBY
Eisenacher Straße 78
Mon-Fri 10:00-18:00;
Sat 10:00-16:00

BOOKS & MUSIC

7 BUCH UND KUNSTANTIQUARIAT TODE
Dudenstraße 36
Mon-Fri 13:00-20:00;
Sat 12:00-16:00

8 DEUKER PIANOS & FLÜGEL
Dudenstraße 36
Wed-Fri 12:00-18:00; Sat 10:00-14:00

9 GAMES&HANDYS. ANKAUF VERKAUF TAUSCH
Kolonnenstraße 66
Mon-Fri 10:00-20:00;
Sat 11:00-19:00

HOME & INTERIORS

10 ANTIK & MODERNE
Belzigerstraße 24
Mon-Fri 12:00-18:00; Sat 11:00-14:00

11 PETERSEN FERNSEHDIENST
Kolonnenstraße 51
Mon-Fri 10:00-20:00;
Sat 10:00-18:00

12 RESTPOSTEN AN + VERKAUF
Dudenstraße 32
Mon-Fri 10:00-20:00;
Sat 11:00-16:00

ONLY IN BERLIN

13 ANTIKFLAIR CAFE&MÖBEL
Grunewaldstraße 10
Mon-Fri 11:00-19:00; Sat 11:00-16:00

14 CAFÉ BILDERBUCH
Akazienstraße 28
Mon-Sat 9:00-24:00;
Sun 10:00-24:00

CHARLOTTENBURG

CLOTHES ◆
BOOKS & MUSIC ◆
HOME & INTERIORS ◆
ONLY IN BERLIN ◆

CLOTHING

1 GARAGE
Ahornstraße 2
Mon-Fri 10:00-19:00; Sat 11:00-18:00

2 MACZY'Z
Mommsenstraße 2
Mon-Fri 12-19 Sa:12 -16

3 MADONNA
Mommsenstraße 57
Mon-Fri 12:00-19:00; Sat 11:00-17:00

4 SECONDO
Mommsenstraße 61
Mon-Fri 11:00-18:30; Sat 11:00-15:30

5 TONY DURANTE
Suarezstraße 62
Mon-Fri 12:00-18:30; Sat 11:30-16:00

HOME & INTERIORS

6 ART+INDUSTRY
Bleibtreustraße 40
Mon-Fri 14:00-18:30; Sat 11:00-16:00

7 HANS-PETER JOCHUM
Bleibtreustraße 41
Mon-Fri 14:00-18:30; Sat 11:00-16:00

8 L&M LEE
Kurfürstendamm 32
Mon-Sat opening at 10:00

9 REISEANTIQUITÄTEN
Suarezstraße 48-49
Mon-Fri 12:00-19:00; Sat 11:00-15:00

10 SCHÖNE ALTE GLÄSER
Suarezstraße 58
Mon-Fri 11:00-18:00; Sat 11:00-15:00

11 ZEITLOS
Kantstraße 17
Mon-Sat 10:00-19:00

ONLY IN BERLIN

12 CLASSIC REMISE. MEILENWERK
Wiebestraße 36-37
Mon-Sat 8:00-20:00;
Sun 10:00-20:00

13 TIERGARTEN
Straße des 17. Juni
Sat-Sun 10:00-17:00

14 UHREN KUNST BISCHOFF
Pestalozzistraße 54
Mon-Fri 13:00-18:00; Sat 10:00-13:00

NEUKÖLLN

CLOTHES ◆
BOOKS & MUSIC ◆
HOME & INTERIORS ◆
ONLY IN BERLIN ◆

CLOTHING

1 **KLEINES GLÜCK**
Weichselstraße 38
Tue-Sat 11:00-17:00

BOOKS & MUSIC

2 **ASA90**
Fuldastraße 55
Tue-Fri 11:00-19:00; Sat 11:00-16:00

3 **BUCHLADEN BUNBURY**
Weserstraße 210
Mon-Fri 11:00-20:00; Sat 11:00-19:00

4 **CITY RAD**
Richardstraße 112
Mon-Fri 10:00-20:00;
Sat 10:00-14:00

5 **DIE BIOGRAFISCHE BIBLIOTHEK**
Richardstraße 55
Mon-Fri 15:00-19:00; closed Wed

6 **FAHRRAD UND MOPEDLADEN**
Pflügerstraße 75
Mon-Fri 9:00-18:00; Sat 9:00-12:00

7 **FITS**
Weichselstraße 59
Tue-Sat 13:00-20:00

8 **GLÜCKSVELO**
Pannierstraße 53a
Tue-Fri 9:00-12:00, 14:00-19:00;
Sat 11:00-16:00

HOME & INTERIORS

9 **ACCESSORIES & AMBIENTE**
Bürknerstraße 39
Mon-Fri 13:00-20:00; Sat 12:00-17:00

10 **ADLER**
Weichselstraße 15
Mon-Sat: 12-20

11 **BERLIN-TRÖDEL**
Pannierstraße 10A
Mon-Sat 10:00-19:00

12 **DAKKOUR ELEKTRONIC**
Erkstraße 21
Mon-Sat 10:00-18:30

13 **EKSTASE 51 LICHT & DESIGN**
Friedelstraße 51
Tue-Fri 15:00-19:00; Sat 14:00-18:00

14 **HAUSHALTSGERÄTE-PETER WIENS**
Sonnenallee 38
Mon-Fri 10:00-18:00; Sat 10:00-14:00

15 **TAMIM**
Hobrechtstraße 6
Mon-Fri 9:00-18:00

ONLY BERLIN

16 **ANTIK & TRÖDELMARKT RICHARDSTRASSE**
Richardstraße 105
Mon-Fri 10:00-18:00

17 **DIE TELLER GOTTES**
Bruno-Bauer-Str. 22
Mon-Fri 11:00-18:00

18 **NOWKÖLLN-FLOWMARKT**
Maybachufer
every 3rd Sunday of the month

19 **SING BLACKBIRD**
Sanderstraße 11
Mon-Sun 10:30-20:00

BERLIN
INDEX OF SHOPS

A

A & V Michaelis 21
A & V Second-Bike 66
A & V Tech 96
A & V Waschbär 94
Accessories & Ambiente 113
Adler 113
Adler Antik 88
Alex Vintage Store 37
Amitola 120
Antik & Moderne 108
Antik & Trodelmarkt Richardstrasse 132
Antike Bauelemente 128
Antikflair Café & Mobel 129
Antik und Buchmarkt am 128
   Bodemuesum
Antik und Trodelmarkt am 121
   Ostbahnhof
Antiquariat in Friedrichshain 66
Antiquariat Kalligram 60
Antiquariat Matthias Wagner 67
Antiquariat Weigelt 67
Antique Vintage Jewellery 38
   Oliver Rheinfrank
Arena Hallen-Trodelmarkt 118
Arkonaplatz Flea Market 123
Art et Antiquities 60
Art + Industry 110
ASA90 80
Audio-In 68
Aunes 48
Aus Zweiter Hand 103

B

Berlin-Trödel 113
Berliner Modeinstitut 21
Bibliotheca Culinaria 70
Bike:Co:Holics 60

Blitz Boutique Berlin 38
Blue Eyes 28
Bötzow Rad Berlin 70
Boxhagener Platz Flea Market 121
Buchladen Bunbury 81
Buch und Kunstantiquariat Tode 78

C

Café Bilderbuch 129
Calypso 39
Cash 40
Checkpoint & Cinema 16
City Rad 81
Classic Remise. Meilenwerk 130
Colours 16
Cou-Cou 28

D

Dakkour Elektronic 114
Das Neue Schwarz 40
Der Möbelladen 96
Deuker Pianos & Flügel 79
Die Biografische Bibliothek 82
Die Teller Gottes 132

E

E-Haus 97
Ekstase 51 Licht & Design 114
Extra-Buch: Modernes Antiquariat 61

F

Fahrrad und Mopedladen 82
Fair Exchange 61
Firlefanz 49
FITS 83, 84
Freak Out Records 70
Friedrichs Lust Schreiber 97
   + Mozedlani

G

Games & Handys. Ankauf Verkauf
Tausch 79
Garage 52
Garments 41
Geile Jacken 22
Glanzstücke 42
Glücksvelo 85
Grünberger An & Verkauf 94
Guerilliaz 88

H

Hammett 61
Hans-Peter Jochum 110
Haushaltsgeräte – Peter Wiens 115
Hilly's Berlin 29
Humana 22

J

Jibboo 23
Jumbo Second Hand 17

K

Kindersachen Aus 2. Hand 17
Klassikerfundus 88
Kleider-Motte 23
Kleines Glück 55, 56-57
Kollwitz Kabinett 100
Komfort 36 89
Kramari 89
Kubi's Bike Shop 62
Kultgut 62
Kunst-A-Bunt 100
Kunst und Antiquitaten 94

L

L & M Lee 111
Lampenmanufaktur Berlin 100
Lindt 18
Long Player – Vinyl Living Room 62
Lumpen Prinzessin 49
Lunettes Brillenagentur 42, 44-45

M

Maczy'z 52
Made in Berlin 43
Madonna 53
Magasin 101
Marheineke Markthalle 118

Mauerpark Flea Market 123
Meins & Deins: The Real Flashback 29
Melting Point 71
Mimi 50
Möbel Kombinat Berlin 101, 98-99
Modern Graphics 63
Mogwa 71
Motz-Der Laden 118
Musikinstrumente & Design 72
Müßiggang 63

N

Nesthocker 90
Nowkölln – Flowmarkt 119
Nyx 30

O

Objets Trouvés. Nonchalantes Wohnen 102
O.F.T. 43
Optiking 30
Original in Berlin 95
Oscar 23
Other Land 64
O-Ton Recordstore 68

P

Paris Second Hand 24
Paul's Boutique Berlin 31
Petersen Fernsehdienst 108
Peter's Werkstatt 119
Philatelie 124, 126-127
Piatto Forte 64
Pira X – Berlin 95
Polsterei & Galerie 90
Pony Hütchen 90

R

Radio Art 120
RAW Flea Market 122
Re-cycle 72
The Recordstore 75, 76-77
Reiseantiquitäten 111
Rembetis 125
Restposten An + Verkauf 109
Rianna in Berlin 46
Rocking Chair 24, 26-27
Rosenrot 18

S

Saint George's	73
St. Prenzl'Berg	73
Satori-Records	64
Schneewitte	32
Schöne Alte Gläser	112
Schönhauser Music I	74
Schubladen	91
Second-Bike und Sound Café An & Verkauf	69
Secondhand	32
Second-Hand Paradise	19
Secondo	53
Sentimental Journey	33
XVII or Dix-Sept	47
Shakespeare and Sons	74
ShöwRaum	91, 92-93
Silhouette im Farbenreigen	50
Sing Blackbird	133
Sir Henri & My Feet	25
Soeur	33, 34-35
Sofortbild Shop Berlin	75
Sommerladen	46
Sozialer Bucherladen	74
Sparbuch	69
ST Store Berlin	19
Steifel Kombinat	36, 98-99
Sterling Gold	47
Stue	104, 106-107
Studio Ziben	102
Stylo	20

T

Tamim	115
Tausendundein Buch	65
Technischer An & Verkauf	96
Thrift Store	36
Tiergarten	131
Tony Durante	54
Trash-Schick	25
Trollby	51
20th Century Interior Berlin	104

U

Uhren & Kunst Bischoff	131
Umbras Kuriositäten-Kabinett	65
Umbras Matthias Wagner	65
Unterwegs	78

VWZ

VEB Orange	125
Waahnsinn	105
Zeitlos	112
Zwischenzeit	103